# 2001
## filming the future

# 2001
## filming the future

**Piers Bizony**

*with a foreword by*
**Arthur C. Clarke**

**AURUM PRESS**

First published in Great Britain in 2000 by

**Aurum Press Limited**
**25 Bedford Avenue**
**London WC1B 3AT**

A catalogue record of this book is available from the British Library.

ISBN 1 85410 706 2

1 3 5 7 9 10 8 6 4 2
2000 2002 2004 2003 2001

Designed by Piers Bizony
Jacket design by Don McPherson

Printed in Spain by Grafos SA, Barcelona

# contents:

# foreword:

## Dr Arthur C. Clarke, C.B.E.

WHEN STANLEY KUBRICK wrote to me in the spring of 1964, saying that he wanted to make the 'proverbial good science-fiction movie', the lunar landing still seemed, psychologically, a dream of the far future. Intellectually, we knew that it was inevitable; emotionally, we could not really believe it—as indeed, some foolish people do not believe it even now.

To put early 1964 in perspective: the *Mercury* Project was complete; the first two-man *Gemini* capsules would not be ready for another year; and argument was still raging about the nature of the lunar surface. The bug-like *Apollo* lunar module was still on the drawing boards. Though there was great activity behind the scenes, and NASA was spending the entire budget of our movie (over $10 million) every *day*, space exploration seemed to be marking time. But the portents were clear. *2001: A Space Odyssey* would still be on its first run while men were actually walking on the Moon.

We had to out-guess the future. One way of doing that was to be so far ahead of the present that there was no danger of facts overtaking us. On the other hand, if we got too far ahead there would be a grave risk of losing contact with our audience. The year 2001 seemed like a good date to choose—and a suitably symbolic one.

Somehow, Stanley and I had to create a story that would not be made obsolete, or even worse, ridiculous, by the events of the next few years. Watching our little movie today, I think that we did pretty well...

True, there are no immediate prospects of building a giant ship like *Discovery* to explore the outer planets. We have yet to conquer Mars, or even to retrace our footsteps on the Moon. But the date in the title of our movie—2001—was never intended as a literal prediction of when such adventures might take place.

In a grim sort of way, it is fascinating to view *2001* in the context of what *hasn't* happened in real life. Our depiction of a huge base constructed on (and partly under) the lunar surface at the end of this decade was, in retrospect, hopelessly optimistic. The central themes of the movie, however, remain entirely valid. We will eventually return to the Moon, then journey to the planets and beyond. It is inevitable. Historians in some far distant future will, no doubt, regard the current half-century delay in our plans as nothing more than temporary, a brief hiccup in the greater span of events.

Let's not get too depressed, though, about our more immediate prospects in space—or indeed, about the great explorations that have already been made. Some things happened far *sooner* than Stanley and I predicted...

We could never have guessed, back in the sixties, that a mission to Jupiter and its moons lay, not in the 21st century, but only fifteen years ahead. Nor could we have imagined the wonders that would be found there. When *2001* was written, Io, Europa, Ganymede and Callisto were mere smudges of light in even the most powerful telescopes. Today we know a great deal more about them—for instance, that Io is the most volcanic world in the entire Solar System, with a surface that puts Dante's *Inferno* to shame. And barely *seven* years elapsed between the first screening of our movie and the beaming of colour images from the surface of Mars. We have mapped the Red Planet almost as thoroughly as the lunar surface—perhaps more so. Mars, Venus, and other distant worlds about which absolutely nothing was known when we first began work on *2001* have since become real places.

In a sense, far from slowing down after the frenetic period of project *Apollo*, space exploration has advanced at an incredible pace. The *Voyager* and *Viking* missions weren't quite the same, perhaps, as sending astronauts in giant ships like our *Discovery*, but they got the job done, and on a sensible budget. *Voyager* flew past Jupiter (using exactly the same 'perturbation manoeuvre' I described in the novel of *2001*) and then to Saturn and Neptune, before leaving the Solar System altogether—the first man-made object ever to head for the stars. (An inscribed plaque and a special laser disc attached to the vehicle await the inspection of Anybody Out There.)

Which brings me neatly around to the subject of sequels. For more than a decade after the publication of *2001* I swore I would never write a sequel. The *Voyager* missions changed my mind. Science fact was turning out to be much more exciting than science fiction, and I wanted a chance to catch up. My novel *2010: Odyssey Two* (and the movie by Peter Hyams) was about the *real* Jovian system, which was awkward because, in the earlier novel, the spaceship *Discovery* went on to Saturn...

In the movie of *2001*, Stanley wisely avoided confusion by heading straight for Jupiter; besides which, the special effect department was having difficulty producing a convincing Saturnian ring system. In the event, *Voyager*'s pictures showed the rings to be more complex than we could ever have put onto screen, with not just dozens, but thousands of strands; some of them braided around each other by gravitational forces of extraordinary complexity. Yes, I'm positively *glad* Stanley and I never made it to Saturn (though I think we did a very respectable job with Jupiter).

I abandoned Saturn in my novels *2010* and *2061: Odyssey Three*, partly to remain consistent with the movie, but more because I wanted to explore Jupiter myself, in the wake of *Voyager*'s stunning images. I make no apology for these inconsistencies.

Anyway—here is an excellent account of how we made the movie. Before handing you over to *2001: Filming the Future*, I would like to congratulate Piers Bizony. I really applaud his long labour of love in producing this book. Thanks, also, to Simon Atkinson, whose painstaking recreations of *2001*'s spacecraft designs are an invaluable contribution.

*Just recently, I dreamed that Stanley and I were talking together. He was looking exactly the same as he did in 1964, when I first knew him. He turned to me and asked: 'Well, Arthur? What shall we do next?'*

*For the last three decades, I always felt there really might have been a 'next', but when I received the shocking and completely unexpected news that Stanley had died suddenly at the age of 70, I knew, with great sorrow, that he and I would not be able to welcome the year 2001 together. I shall miss him.*

**A.C.C.**
**Colombo**
**April 28, 2000**

# author's note:

I FIRST SAW Stanley Kubrick's *2001: A Space Odyssey* in September 1968, at the age of nine. I was taken to a cinema in Horsham, in rural Sussex, to see what was supposed to be the grandest film about space exploration that had ever been made. I was looking forward to smart young space cadets in sleek rocketships, conquering the galaxy.

The film began well: a sunrise in space, and some loud, exciting music. Ten minutes later, I began to feel bored and disappointed. I thought the ape sequences at the beginning were reels from the wrong film, that the projectionist must have made a mistake. Then that strange and powerful music from the very start of the film came on again, and the ape was swinging a bone and smashing some skulls, which certainly looked like a lot of fun to me.

When the bone went off into space (Kubrick's much-celebrated 'jump cut' from bone tool to nuclear satellite) I felt more excited. *This* was the film I'd nagged my mum and dad to take me to. I watched and watched, and to be honest the precise nature of the plot simply passed me by. I was hooked on the sensory experience, the hardware, the weird and terrifying noises coming out of the screen. I thought, maybe there wasn't a story—that the film was a sort of Planetarium display, like the one next to Madame Tussaud's waxworks, only bigger and better. I didn't understand where the apes had come from, but as soon as the spaceships came on, I was quite happy just to sit back and enjoy the show.

Vividly, I remember how Kubrick's giant space station seemed to tumble over my head. Its gentle rotation against a backdrop of stars was one of the most beautiful things I had ever seen, and I still get a lump in my throat when I see it today. I didn't know the name of the music it seemed to be dancing to—the *Blue Danube* waltz—but I thought it was much better than the usual electronic bleeps and wails you got in other space films. I thought the orbiting station and the other ships looked so real, I could never quite believe they didn't exist.

Later on, in the Jupiter spaceship, the crew ran around the walls, walked upside-down and floated about in the vacuum. It all looked so *real*.

The glowing space baby? Dimly, I was aware that the red-suited astronaut at the end of the film had 'turned into' something. I was used to this sort of thing from *Dr Who* and *Star Trek*, so it wasn't a problem. I supposed, if it was a baby it had to be a 'good' transformation rather than a 'bad' one. Obviously, going into space, you would meet mysterious alien forces and have strange things happen to you.

When we came out of the cinema, my parents were frowning, puzzled. 'Did you enjoy that?' they wanted to know. I spent the journey home in the car rattling off all the things I had enjoyed. 'And did you understand any of it?' they asked me.

I didn't know what they meant.

'You're not supposed to understand it! You're just meant to *watch* it' I blurted out.

I was hurt that my parents were so dissatisfied with what they had seen, and felt slightly guilty for having pestered them for so many days to take me along to a film they clearly hadn't enjoyed. I was also afraid that I'd shown myself up to be stupid, by not having 'understood' the plot. If mum and dad said there was supposed to be a story in it, then I must have missed something.

Of course, so had they.

Looking back, I think that similar scenes must have been acted out between parents and children across the length and breadth of the cinema-going world in that summer of 1968, as far as *2001* was concerned. Of course, other, more serious battles between different generations were unfolding in London, Paris and at Kent State University, but I was too young to take in much of that. *2001*'s widely differing reception from young and adult audiences is now acknowledged, however, as thoroughly representative of the great rifts between parents and their children in artistic, political and moral perception which so shaped the late 1960s. I may have been too young to stand behind the barricades, but I understood, as my parents never could, that *2001* was something different and important; not a 'normal' film at all, but a kind of visual fairground ride; not a work of art just to go and look at, but a *place to visit.*

All through my teenage years—with their endless distractions, their natural preoccupations—certain images from *2001* stayed with me. In 1977 the film was re-released on the back of publicity for George Lucas's *Star Wars*, and I had a chance to reappraise it with an older and marginally wiser mind. Reading the library copies of 1968 newspaper reviews and articles about the film, I saw at last that my childhood judgement had been essentially correct. 'You're just meant to *watch* it!'

I never saw anything like *2001* again, and never understood why the science fiction films of the mid-1970s were so unambitious by comparison. In recent years directors like Stephen Spielberg and Ridley Scott have done much to reinvigorate the genre, but I would still argue that the boldness, the originality, of *2001* hasn't really been matched; and few cinema visions of the future have managed to remain quite so plausible after so long a time. Most of the space films of the early 1970s, for instance, look hopelessly dated. It is striking that *2001*'s predictions still seem forward-looking as we approach the year 2001 itself.

Now, unbelievably, a third of a century has passed since the film's first release, and this 'futuristic' epic has become a venerable kind of museum piece, an antiquity. For three years I engaged upon a kind of archaeology—an archaeology of the future, and of the past. I tried to locate artifacts from the film's production effort. I triggered the memories of some of the principal creative staff. I studied fading film stills in cinema archives and photographic libraries; meanwhile, my colleagues and collaborators put in even greater efforts, unearthing all kinds of treasures, gradually revealing the echoes of a bold 1960s Modernist vision of the future that seems as distant from us today as the world of ancient Egypt—and no less fascinating.

Unlike so many other space films, *2001* isn't simply a casual product of cinematic imagination. The arbitrariness of so much science fiction design is entirely absent here. This is, *literally*, how the engineers and scientists of the time saw their future developing. The film has a kind of honorary reality, and its design details are just as valid for historical reference today as are the equivalent details of real artifacts from the past. We can study the thoughts and inventions of Kubrick's much-vaunted 'space experts' with the same high seriousness with which we might consider the building of an ancient Greek trireme or a wooden battleship of the Trafalgar era. We can look at all the beautiful artifacts in the film and learn, not so much about the year 2001, but the world of 1968.

This latest edition of my book has been made possible by the continuing generosity of the many people who helped me first time around, along with several new and equally generous contributors. I thank them all, and I hope that history will judge our collective effort worthwhile. (A properly detailed list of everyone involved with this book appears on page 165.)

**Piers Bizony**

For Release Tuesday, February 23, 1965

                    STANLEY KUBRICK TO FILM
                  "JOURNEY BEYOND THE STARS"
                     IN CINERAMA FOR MGM

   Stanley Kubrick, who received world-wide acclaim as the director of
"Lolita" and most recently "Dr. Strangelove," will bring "Journey Beyond
the Stars" to the screen for Metro-Goldwyn-Mayer. The picture, which will
begin production on August 16th with a cast of international importance,
will be filmed in the Cinerama process, and in color. The announcement was
made in New York today (23) by MGM President Robert H. O'Brien.

   Based on a novel to be published this winter by Arthur C. Clarke and
Stanley Kubrick, "Journey Beyond the Stars" will be filmed on locations
in Britain, Switzerland, Africa, Germany and the United States. Interior
scenes will be filmed at the MGM Studio in London. The screenplay for
the production will be written by Kubrick and Clarke.

   Describing the production, Kubrick stated:

   " 'Journey Beyond the Stars' is an epic story of adventure and exploration, encompassing the Earth, the planets of our Solar System, and a journey light-years away to another part of the Galaxy. It is a scientifically-
based yet dramatic attempt to explore the infinite possibilities that
space travel now opens to mankind. The great biologist J.B.S. Haldane
said: 'The Universe is not only stranger than we imagine; it is stranger
than we _can_ imagine.' When you consider that in our Galaxy there are a
hundred _billion_ stars, of which our Sun is a perfectly average specimen,
and that present estimates put the number of Galaxies in the visible
Universe at a hundred _million_, Haldane's statement seems rather conserva-
tive.

   "Space is one of the great themes of our age, yet, it is one still almost untouched in serious art and literature."

   "Now that the first man-carrying spaceships are actually being built,

from METRO-GOLDWYN-MAYER 1540 BROADWAY, N.Y.C. 10036 · JUDSON 2-2000 OT SUBD, LRAB, RTA-B, SS, NMA-B, NRT

(2)

and the United States is spending over $10,000,000 a day to reach the Moon, and robot probes have already been launched to Mars and Venus, it is time to break away from the cliches of Monsters and Madmen. There will be dangers in space---but there also will be wonder, adventure, beauty, opportunity, and sources of knowledge that will transform our civilization, as the voyages of the Renaissance brought about the end of the Dark Ages.

"During the last few years, some of the world's best minds have applied themselves to questions such as: Since we are about to explore space, has anyone already visited Earth? If so, did they come 100, 1,000 or 1,000,000 years ago? Does intelligent life exist on other planets of this Sun, such as Mars or Venus---or will we have to span the million-times greater distance to the other stars before we encounter intelligent beings?

"The story of 'Journey Beyond the Stars' opens in the year 2001, when permanent bases have been established on the moon, manned expeditions have visited Mars, and automatic probes have been sent to all the major planets of this Solar System. Enough has been discovered to make it certain that only the Earth, of all the Sun's children, has ever brought forth intelligence; there are simple life forms on Mars, but that is all. Mankind is alone in the Solar System.

"Then, unexpectedly, and from uncomfortably close at hand, comes the electrifying discovery of extra-terrestrial intelligence."

Clarke is credited in official Communications Satellite Corporation histories as the first person to describe in detail, in Wireless World, October 1945, the communications satellite system. He has written 29 fiction and non-fiction works in addition to "Man and Space," which he wrote in collaboration with the Editors of Life Magazine. Currently engaged in underwater photography on the Great Barrier Reef of Australia and the coast of Ceylon, Clarke is President of the Ceylon Astronomical Society and Past Chairman of the British Interplanetary Society. In 1961 he was awarded the UNESCO-Kalinga £1,000 Prize and in 1963 the Stuart Ballantine Gold Medal (Franklin Institute).

———

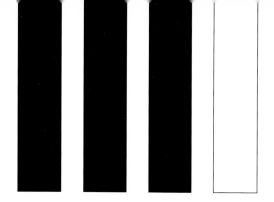

# 1 : the ultimate trip

UNTIL THE 1960s, science-fiction films had been part of the 'B' movie stock-in-trade. Rockets built out of cardboard tubes shuddered across sets made from tin foil and egg cartons; Christmas tree lights bolted onto tea chests doubled as flashing computer consoles; and intrepid explorers really did wander around with goldfish bowls over their heads. Very few production companies imagined that space fiction adventures might be capable of attracting adults into the movie theatres. Such adventures were kids' stuff; and in the 1950s, young people weren't necessarily the dominant marketing target in Hollywood, the way they are today. Nobody was prepared to spend millions of dollars to entertain *them*. Certain studios churned out vast numbers of monster-horror features as cheaply as possible, for the benefit of the teenage drive-in audiences (of course, a great many of these fantasies were designed for young couples *not* to have to pay too much attention to). In general though, Hollywood spent the serious money on developing more traditional themes.

But by 1961 Russia had sent real astronauts into orbit, riding on giant rockets which actually worked. Buck Rogers suddenly became a very grown-up concern: a matter to be taken very seriously by politicians, generals and taxpayers. The Hollywood cardboard looked distinctly limp in comparison to the real thing.

In May 1961, President John F. Kennedy made a dramatic speech designed to divert the American public's attention away from their own rocket programme's humiliating series of false starts. Time and again, the Soviets seemed to be beating them in the space arena. 'I believe that this nation should commit itself to the goal, before this decade is out, of landing a man on the Moon and returning him safely to Earth,' he challenged. Stirring stuff indeed, as the Soviets blasted heavy capsules ever more confidently into stable orbits, while the first tiny American *Mercury* vehicles did little more than poke their stubby noses above the atmosphere for half an orbit or so, before falling back to Earth.

And thus the 'Moon Race' began. Out of purely strategic political brinksmanship, humankind's greatest single achievement emerged. Newborn NASA was geared to reaching the Moon first, at virtually any cost, in the nine slender years that remained until the Presidential deadline ran out. (Kennedy's tragic assassination only two years later made the task seem even more urgent.) NASA rapidly expanded to become America's seventh-largest government department. Nearly 40,000 staffers worked on various rocket projects out of huge compounds scattered right across the country; and by the middle of 1965 there were 300,000 contractor employees, in any number of aerospace and electronics companies, fabricating

**Preceding pages:**
*This is the original MGM press release which first announced to the world that Stanley Kubrick had turned his attention to outer space.*

components for the huge and complex *Saturn* and *Apollo* moon vehicles. It was impossible for Hollywood to ignore this vast undertaking. More and more potential movie-goers were staying at home, watching live broadcasts from Cape Kennedy, as the USA started to gain its own faltering successes. Clean-cut young heroes were shown being strapped into complicated capsules, and then blasting up toward the stars atop giant pillars of flame.

This was the stuff that dreams were made of. Television dreams... Hollywood was losing out to Walter Cronkite reporting direct from NASA on TV. It was losing out to *I Love Lucy*, or the *Johnny Carson Show*. Comedians and astronauts now had centre stage (while Vietnam fretted and fumed in the wings, rehearsing its own blood-soaked script).

In the summer of 1964, a young and highly talented film maker approached the MGM production company with an idea. New York-born director Stanley Kubrick had just scored a big critical and commercial hit with *Dr Strangelove: or How I Learned to Stop Worrying and Love the Bomb*. It was a brilliant spoof on the Cold War, in which Peter Sellers played a variety of characters, including the mad German strategic adviser Dr Strangelove, spouting the gospel of world destruction from his wheelchair. In the wake of the Cuban Missile Crisis, the film struck a welcome chord with a nervous, fatalistic public.

As is the way in Hollywood, a director who scores a smash hit gets to write his own cheques, for one more movie at least. Kubrick told his potential backers at MGM that he intended his next project to be the best and most realistic space adventure ever made. It would deal with our immediate future in space, and would portray our first contact with beings from another world. The screenplay would capitalize on widescale interest in the forthcoming *Apollo* moonshots. The foremost British science fiction writer Arthur C. Clarke would join him, to help shape a truly convincing and detailed scenario.

Kubrick stated that he planned on spending two years and $6 million of MGM's precious time and money. The studio was certainly keen on the idea in principle, because rival studios were already starting to put moderately-budgeted space films into production. But they were aghast at the figures and timescales Kubrick had in mind. They were being asked to fund not just the most expensive SF film ever made, but one of the most expensive films of *any* kind ever made. $6 million was a very large amount of money back then. True enough, Richard Burton and Elizabeth Taylor had succeeded in spending far more than that on their epic *Cleopatra*, but it was a massive financial disaster with an expense sheet thirty years ahead of its time. Kubrick's $6 million was about the highest stack of cash that Hollywood was capable of climbing. His fiscal requirements would push at the very edges of the financial safety margin for a single film project.

The ancient Hollywood rules applied, however: if MGM didn't give hotshot Stanley what he wanted, somebody else probably would. So they agreed. MGM's chief executive Robert O'Brien authorized funding. Kubrick and Clarke had already spent more than six months in New York researching and outlining a draft screenplay for presentation to their backers, and on February 23, 1965, O'Brien announced that his studio would finance *Journey Beyond the Stars*. (This 'working title' was never a serious contender.) The plan was to release Kubrick's completed movie at the end of 1966, or by spring 1967 at the latest.

In the event, Kubrick's epic was more than three years in the making, not two; and it came in at an officially quoted budget of well over $10 million. O'Brien spent those years fighting off the criticisms of his stockholders, as Kubrick's budget climbed and time dragged on. And when at last, at the end of March 1968, MGM executives got to preview what they had put their money into—*2001: A Space Odyssey*—they couldn't decide if they were looking at the biggest financial disaster in MGM's history, or at one of the greatest movies ever made...

The official budget had little to do with the *real* cost of completing *2001*. Kubrick's epic swallowed up most of the resources of the MGM London production lot at Borehamwood for three years: nine shooting stages were all heavily booked for the same project, along with occasional spells at Elstree and Shepperton,

***A match for Kubrick's intellect:***
*Arthur C. Clarke in the pod bay
set. 'One of the most fruitful and
rewarding collaborations I have
had was with Arthur Clarke,'
Stanley Kubrick said of him.*

during a time when, under more favourable conditions, the studio could have expected to churn out ten or twelve major features from that facility. They only put out half that number. As *2001* was shot in MGM's own studios, many of the basic overheads of running and maintaining the vast complex were not factored into the quoted budget. Ordinarily, this might have been little more than a problem for the 'creative accountants'. Three years, however, is a long time for a studio facility to spend *not* making other films. O'Brien was under great pressure. By 1967 the British studio lots were enough of a liability already. Now that Hollywood's general monopoly over the entertainment business was losing out to TV, maintaining expensive lots abroad was increasingly difficult. And anyway, back home, MGM was drifting into debt on its own account.

However, against the advice of friends and enemies alike, MGM's chief gave Kubrick all the support he needed. The director had persuaded him that it would all be worth it in the end. Though he was first and foremost a businessman, Robert O'Brien believed in movies for their own sake (literally *Ars Gratia Artis*, as the MGM motto went). Roger Caras, in charge of *2001*'s publicity campaign, remembers that 'Bob O'Brien believed in Stanley, it was that simple. When you consider the role he had to play as president of a major Hollywood studio, O'Brien was a remarkably pleasant man. Unlike so many of them, he wasn't jaded. He could be a believer.' Stanley Kubrick has acknowledged the debt of honour he owes to O'Brien, who always had faith in the true value of *2001*. Certainly when O'Brien saw the early sequences emerging from the tight security of the studio, he recognized that something extraordinary was shaping up. Even the executives at his back, knives out, were stunned by the images Kubrick was coming up with. But they never imagined that the final cut of the film would be so... well, so... *confusing*.

At the press previews in Washington, Los Angeles and New York during late March and early April 1968, the critics were equally puzzled. Obviously, what was on screen represented an incredible technical achievement, they were all agreed about that. But just what kind of a movie *was* this? It didn't seem to have any beginning, any middle, or any proper ending. Nobody even *spoke* in it for the first half-hour! There were apemen waving bones which turned suddenly into spaceships. There was a giant human foetus that didn't seem to have much reason for being there. The main human characters had less personality than insurance salesmen. There was a deranged red-eyed computer. There were aliens that looked like black slabs of rock which kept cropping up, again for no discernable reason. What did it all mean? Where was the story? What had Kubrick done with the *plot*?

Reviewers had gone into the screening rooms expecting a traditional drama of human crisis, love, hate, battle and resolution up among the stars. What they got was one man's obsessively detailed, multi-million-dollar waking dream of humankind's evolutionary and technological destiny. 'An epic achievement,' said *Life* magazine's reviewer, writing pretty much on auto-pilot (*Life* had committed a six-page colour spread to publicizing the project); while Renata Adler wrote with greater conviction in *The New York Times* that *2001* 'is so completely absorbed in its own problems, its fanatical devotion to detail, that it is somewhere between hypnotic and immensely boring.' In a rare error of judgement, the great Pauline Kael described *2001* in her *Harpers'* magazine article as a 'monumentally unimaginative' piece of work. (There are those who will testify that Kael's nasty review upset Kubrick considerably.) Meanwhile, *Variety*—never the most generous judge— suggested that *2001* might be lucky enough 'to do biz on initial release,' but summed up Kubrick's epic as 'plodding... confusing.' The film's strange mix of gleaming technology, god-like aliens and petty human insignificance was too much for most critics. Some of them appreciated the complex special effects; but just as many felt confused, irritated and bored.

Part of the problem may have been that the film was nearly two and three-quarter hours long at that point. After the first showings, Kubrick trimmed nineteen minutes from the running time: mainly from the routine sequences of docking, spacewalks and so on. He made these cuts entirely of his own accord. *2001* remains the film which he wanted us to see all along; it's still the 'Director's Cut'. Those who have suggested that his cuts were a 'panic reaction' should keep in mind that old adage: 'a work of art is never finished, only abandoned'. One of his production colleagues has joked that 'If MGM hadn't pretty much torn that movie out of Stanley's hands, he'd still be working on it today.' Kubrick prowled up and down the aisles at the premiere, assessing the audience's 'squirm factor'. In several interviews he has said that he hardly had time to see the finished film himself before its release. He was still editing in a specially converted suite on board the *Queen Elizabeth* as it carried him across the Atlantic. He simply saw a few places in the film where he could 'tighten things up a bit.'

The only really significant cut was a sequence in which Hal powers down the radio in Poole's pod, before turning the little repair capsule into a murder weapon. Hence Dave Bowman's question, 'Have you made radio contact with him yet?' To which Hal replies with pedantic truthfulness, 'The radio is still dead.' A visually stunning scene showing David Bowman rootling about in a storage corridor for a spare antenna control unit was also eliminated. Apart from these snips, the most important alteration wasn't so much a cut, but an addition. Audiences were having trouble working out the connection between the mysterious black slab and the apeman Moonwatcher's sudden interest in bones. Kubrick inserted a half-second 'flashback' to the black slab, as though Moonwatcher were dimly remembering it.

Moonwatcher wasn't really called that in the movie, of course. That was Arthur C. Clarke's name for him. Even then world-famous for his highly literate science fiction stories, Clarke had provided a framework of child-like wonder, of travel to the far planets, and meetings with benevolent beings from another world. He had defined fresh possibilities for mystical experience in a technological age which had forgotten how to search its own soul. But Kubrick scattered this hopeful vision with a unique and discomforting reminder that such adventures might cost us more than we bargained for. The triumph of the human intellect, he seemed to say, would be achieved only by sacrificing all

that we hold to be most human about being human. Even so, the director's cynicism about the modern condition—his ghastly astronauts, with their pallid faces, their chilling lack of communication—was tempered, without the slightest sense of irony, with one of cinema's most extraordinary images of hope and wonder: the benevolent, wide-eyed starchild at the film's end, all wisdom and compassion. This, at least, is Clarkean optimism in full swing. (The starchild is a more poignant image than most of us have ever realized, as we shall see toward the end of this book.)

*2001* was unapologetically ambiguous. It seemed to offer catastrophe and redemption in the same breath. It was unbearably slow, yet deeply thrilling. It was sexless, emotionless, cold, yet weirdly sensuous, debauched in rich colours, awash with swirling shapes and mechanistic eroticism. There was little action, yet tremendous things happened (though exactly *what* things, nobody was quite sure). The soundtrack was also quite startling. Kubrick made brilliant use of music, and paid the closest attention to such things as the air-conditioning hiss inside a spaceship, or the rumbling of its mechanical components. He turned the microphones onto the breathing of an astronaut in his helmet. He detailed all the cockpits and control rooms with tiny subtleties of machine noise, and concentrated on the sound made by a chair scraping across a polished floor. And sometimes he would just leave the soundtrack out altogether, allowing the audience to listen to the terrifying silence of deep space, to the vast inhuman nothingness between worlds.

There was also a vast inhuman nothingness between the *people* in the film. The dialogue was almost entirely redundant. Whenever anyone spoke, it was only to say nothing: *Did you have a pleasant flight? Yes, very nice, thanks... Well—anybody hungry? How about a little coffee? Great idea... How's everything going? Fine thank you. We have no complaints. Well, I'm glad to hear it...* The characters spent most of their time being icily polite to each other, without so much as once saying anything significant. The only exception to this was HAL 9000, a talking computer with a glowing red eye. Though his voice was just as calm and level as a

**Kubrick in command:**
*'When it comes to film-making, he's the best,' Arthur C. Clarke said of him.*

wine steward's at an expensive restaurant, he carried within him all the strengths and frailties audiences might have expected to detect in the 'people'. He was prideful, talkative, capable of deception, and burdened with hidden insecurites. This machine mind was more human than human, and thus doubly doomed to kill and be killed. But Kubrick's moral, evolutionary and mythical exploration of men and man-like machines in conflict was too subtle, or too bitter for most reviewers to take on board.

The critics could barely restrain themselves. They rushed off to their typewriters and wrote page after page of vitriol, or worse still, of mindlessly superficial praise. *2001* generated more column-inches of magazine and newspaper verbiage than just about any other film of its era. Part of the reason was that everybody had been waiting for it for so long. This wasn't just another film. It was a cinematic *event*.

Many commentators could not understand how *2001* could make any kind of sense, with all its contradictions, and its apparently crippling lack of ordinary narrative. And what they could not understand, they were determined to destroy. The public, however, was ready to appreciate it at a deeper level, as a cinematic experience to be 'felt' intuitively, rather than to be picked to pieces scene by scene like most conventional dramas. The profound psycho-religious imagery was not lost on the youthful counter-culture of 1968, even if it did leave fifty-year-old critics way behind. This was a film 'for groovin', not for understandin',' according to the common wisdom. (They might have done well to read Penelope Gilliatt in the *New Yorker*, who got the point first time, and wrote a review that was almost as intelligent as the film itself. She grooved it *and* understood it.) As one rueful critic had to admit, some months after 'panning' the film, 'Everybody hates *2001*, except people.'

The shock of getting it so wrong sent reviewers back to their clattering typewriters. *2001* was unusual in that many writers felt the need to review it again, differently, after they had witnessed how the film was affecting the public. Most cinema 'experts' were used to analysing films that were like stage plays—people sitting in rooms and talking to each other, one scene after another. Kubrick's idea of cinema was that

it should be about seeing, as well as listening. What was the point of spending huge sums of money on brilliant photography, if people were not prepared to *look* at what was up there on screen? Traditional movie critics were just theatre critics in disguise. It was time they learned to open their eyes.

MGM benefited enormously from the fact that it was widely regarded as essential to go and see *2001* several times in order to appreciate it properly. Movie-goers thought nothing of queuing up three or four times a week for repeat viewings. ('*2001*? I see it every week,' quipped John Lennon.) Much of the appeal derived from the film's spectacular Cinerama wide-screen process, seen to best effect in the major theatres equipped with appropriate projectors. The whirling shapes on the giant curved screen engulfed whole audiences, already beaten into submission by the noisy wailing from the multi-channel stereo soundtrack.

Kubrick's 'Space Oddity' turned out to be one of MGM's four most famous and successful creations, along with *Gone with the Wind*, *The Wizard of Oz*, and *Doctor Zhivago*. Some theatres kept *2001* on its first run for nearly two years solid, as its reputation grew; and it was re-released twice, very successfully, during the seventies. American receipts amounted to $25 million, with the rest of the world topping that figure up to more than $40 million. Even accounting for inflation, this doesn't seem quite so dramatic as *Star Wars*' $175 million, set against a 1977 budget of $10 million. George Lucas's budget stretched a far shorter distance than had Kubrick's, thanks largely to the oil crisis of the early seventies and the subsequent recession. *Star Wars* was regarded as a remarkably cheap and profitable project, whereas *2001* had been heralded as a remarkably expensive one. What a difference a decade makes... But movie theatre tickets were much cheaper in 1968 than they were ten years later. *2001*'s $40 million represented a lot of theatre rentals, and a lot of backsides on seats.

More recently, *Terminator 2* (1991), *Jurassic Park* (1993) and *Titanic* (1998) came in as the most expensive films ever made, with quoted budgets of about a hundred million, and box

***A discreet facade:***
*The frontage of MGM's studio facility in leafy Borehamwood in 1966 gives nothing away about the spaceships and hardware taking shape within. (Kubrick's office was in this part of the building.)*

office receipts of half a *billion* dollars and more. They won't remain the most costly projects for long. The budgets, and the required profits, seem more unreal than the films themselves. It is almost impossible to make sensible comparisons between a modern studio executive's balance sheet, and the equivalent sheet a quarter of a century ago. The world has changed far too much. At a good guess, it would take something approaching the resources allocated for *Terminator 2* in order to film a project on the scale of *2001* today.

Comparisons aside, *2001* was, in general terms, a big hit by the standards of its time. Even so, the MGM financiers would much rather have recouped their original investment instantly, if not sooner. The first thirty days of the film's release were slower than had been anticipated. There was a feeling among some studio executives that the film should be 'pulled' from the Cinerama houses in favour of MGM's other main contender for that season, *Ice Station Zebra*. The problem was that they had tried to market Kubrick's movie as family entertainment, a rip-roaring adventure, when, of course, it wasn't that kind of movie at all. For very young children and their unprepared parents, *2001* must have been a very confusing experience. By and large, only audiences at least partially primed in advance to the movie's cerebral demands could emerge from the cinemas completely satisfied with what they had seen. Young college students, fresh from discussing Marshall McLuhan in their Media Studies groups, were perfect cannon fodder for Kubrick's grandiose audio-visual experiment. Earnestly discussing it among themselves, they 'primed' the next batch of audiences to go and see it; or else, somewhat less dialectically, they treated the whole thing as an extention of their drug-taking hobbies, buying up what were traditionally the most unpopular seats in the theatres—right up on the front row, uncomfortably close to the huge screen—and then 'turning on, tuning in and dropping out,' to the accompaniment of Kubrick's noisy lightshow (with additional special effects, courtesy of Professor Timothy Leary's chemistry lessons).

Big-budget movies like *2001* were supposed to attract young and old alike—family audiences. Many cinema managers feared that *2001* was a commercial catastrophe right from day one, because advance bookings seemed dangerously low. What they didn't take into account was that twenty-year-olds in 1968 just didn't *do* stuff like that: make advance reservations, flash credit cards and so on. The bulk of *2001*'s box-office receipts were cash sales at the time of screening. For the Hollywood financial analysts and public relations experts of the day, this trend was so unusual that it confused them completely for a while. It wasn't the publicists or the reviewers, but word-of-mouth among younger college student audiences which gradually started filling the movie theatres. *2001* made a handsome profit *in the end*.

But it was already too late for MGM. By 1969 they had accumulated debts of more than $80 million. Despite persistent rumours to the contrary, this wasn't just because of the money they had spent on *2001*. It was part of a far wider financial crisis. Thus weakened, the MGM lion was toothless in its desperate battle to defend itself against corporate raiding. The rapacious and colourful Las Vegas entrepreneur Kirk Kerkorean swallowed the stricken beast whole. That was effectively the end of the old studio as a major creative force in American culture. *2001: A Space Odyssey* was one of their final significant achievements.

Nor was MGM the only one of the great studios in crisis as the turbulent sixties drew to a close. Wall Street bankers were no longer so eager to accommodate their West Coast movie cousins. All Hollywood was in trouble, as television chewed remorselessly into their markets. Indeed, all America was in trouble, as Vietnam came in from the wings at last and took centre stage, making a cruel mockery of the national self-esteem. An era of comparative innocence was coming to an end.

*2001: A Space Odyssey* is as much about the era in which it was made as it is about the future. Kubrick's philosophical exploration was coloured in, so to speak, by the industrial expertise of a great nation at the height of its powers. By the time it was released, the USA was no longer quite so sure of itself—or, indeed,

of its desire to build cities on the Moon by the end of the century. The war in South East Asia burned up vast chunks of taxpayers' money; spaceflight and all its related toys no longer seemed quite so important. NASA started talking rather less about the 'conquest' of space, or the 'colonization' of the planets. In such uncertain times, those sorts of phrase were no longer deemed proper.

The young audiences who so much appreciated Kubrick's spectacular images in the summer of 1968 were in a less receptive mood a year later. Too many of their contemporaries were on the run from the draft, or else were coming home in body bags. They couldn't understand why their friends were being killed in some godforsaken little country half a world away (and their parents couldn't understand why the USA couldn't just win the damn war and get it over with).

*2001* was filmed almost entirely in MGM's British studios at Borehamwood, tucked away deep in suburban north London. Stanley Kubrick shut himself away in his vast palace of optical splendours, like some mythical philosopher king, and generated a vision of the near future which, to a great extent, was being made redundant by current events even as his cameras rolled. Outside the studio, the world turned, the world changed. Kubrick ignored it, and got on with what he was doing. For three years, nobody heard him talk about anything except his film. (Or maybe once: during the Arab-Israeli conflict of 1967 one of his aides heard him mutter something about, 'Where are the Russian advisers? Where are the Russian advisers?,' before turning his mind back to the more important business at hand.)

Today, Kubrick's epic space drama stands as the epitome of science fiction film-making, and as an extraordinary exercise in totally visual cinema. Though history has dented the film's slightly naïve technological optimism, it still represents a dazzling manifesto for our future in space. One day, humankind may be in a position to revive its long-held dream of reaching out to the stars. *2001: A Space Odyssey* will be a useful source of inspiration for many years to come. It's not just about spaceships, about *how* we might travel into space. It's also about *why*.

**Yesterday's tomorrow:**
*Viewed today, '2001' tells us as much about 1968's idea of the future as it does about the year 2001 itself. Real-life NASA cabins and docking corridors are not so smartly designed as Kubrick and his artists imagined they would be (left). The target of futuristic optimism has shifted now from space hardware to the less tangible electronic realm of software designers and the Worldwide Web.*

# 2001: filming the future

Arthur C. Clarke's innovative novel, published with great success shortly after the film's release, still sells in tens of thousands all around the world—a testament, surely, to the continuing interest which *2001* is capable of generating.

At the Oscar ceremonies in the spring of 1969, the significant awards went to Carol Reed's *Oliver!* (Best Film, Best Director, Best Music), to Mel Brook's *The Producers* (Best Original Screenplay) and to *The Lion In Winter* (Best Adapted Screenplay). Far worse, *Planet of the Apes* got a special award for Best Achievement in Makeup, which was a particularly savage blow to Kubrick's production crew after their quite incredible work on the apeman outfits. Although nominated in just about every category, *2001: A Space Odyssey* picked up just one Oscar, for Best Visual Effects.

That season's award winners weren't bad movies, by any means. But in such a tumultuous Time of Revolution, they were hardly revolutionary.

Can *2001* still be regarded as a remarkable film? Yes, almost certainly. If some scenes in the movie appear dated, they are remarkably few. The spaceships still look superb, and the central themes remain as powerful today as they were when audiences first confronted them a quarter of a century ago. Hardware and visual thrills apart, Kubrick's astral epic is a movie of *ideas*. Such intelligence never dates. It will take the passing of many more generations of human explorers before the questions raised by *2001* are answered, and the film becomes redundant at last.

In 1968, Stanley Kubrick summed up the principal intentions of his film thus:

*If 2001 has stirred your emotions, your subconscious, your mythological leanings, then it has succeeded.*

It is still succeeding.

**The poster art:**
*Robert McCall's famous painting shows the space station releasing a shuttle. Later posters for the re-release of the film concentrated on the more abstract Starchild imagery.*

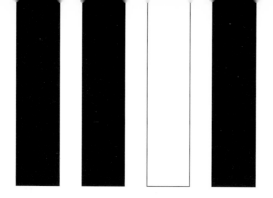

# 2: synopsis

## the dawn of man

FOUR MILLION YEARS AGO, a tribe of primitive apemen struggles to survive in an arid, unforgiving landscape. They huddle together at night for warmth and comfort, while leopards and other savage hunters prowl outside the entrance to the cave where they shelter. Every day is a battle against death, against hunger, against other apeman tribes competing for food, water and territory.

One morning, a strange and frightening object appears in the clearing near their cave. It is a vertical slab, made out of something very black and very smooth. Its shape and its texture are completely unlike anything the apes have ever experienced before. At first, the mood among the troupe is little short of panic. But after a short while the mysterious black stone seems to exert a calming influence on them. They move closer. Curiosity begins to overcome their fear.

The Sun and the Moon reach high in the sky. The apes are unnaturally calm, now. The 'Monolith' is doing its unearthly work.

Next day, the black slab has vanished as suddenly and mysteriously as it arrived. But it has left the traces of its influence deep within the mind of one of our ancestors. If he had a name, it would be 'Moonwatcher', for he is in the habit of staring up at the night sky, at the bright circle of the Moon. He is distinctly brighter and fitter than the other apes, and leader of the troupe. An edge of cunning has placed him above his rivals in the harsh competition for life's advantages.

The Monolith has singled him out.

The sun rises on yet another day of hunger and fear. The apes set off on the urgent business of foraging for whatever nourishment they can find. The slab has already been forgotten; and anyway, this is a time long before memory, long before history. They only have the capacity to concentrate on the here-and-now.

But Moonwatcher is sitting on his haunches next to the skeleton of a large animal, killed, no doubt, by some creature much more powerful and more fearsome than himself—probably by one of the leopards of which the troupe lives in such constant fear. Moonwatcher's gaze is fixed on one of the large, heavy thigh bones. He picks it up and senses its weight in his furry hand. He lets it fall, and the heavy tip of the bone lands with a crunching impact on some other fragment of the dismembered skeleton.

There is *something* here which Moonwatcher feels compelled to try and understand. (The Monolith is still doing its work.) It's a huge intellectual challenge, but Moonwatcher at last begins to see what this bone is, what it can be,

what *he* can make it do. He smashes it down on the skeleton, more confident now with every swing. The skull of the carcass beneath him shatters as the hapless fallen animal dies a second time, in a rehearsal for the many new deaths to come. Deaths that will feed the apemen.

Again and again Moonwatcher hurls down the tip of his bone cudgel. Now, he is more powerful than any creature before him. For the time being, the Monolith's work is complete.

Another dawn, another day, and yet another search for food and water. But today is different. The whole troupe has bone cudgels in imitation of their leader. They have hunted and they have killed. For the first time in many generations there is enough fresh meat to go around. The constant threat of starvation is receding.

But this new triumph involves more than a hint of corruption, of innocence destroyed. The meat in the apemen's bloodied paws attracts a festering swarm of flies.

Another day, and another wearisome dispute with a rival troupe over the local water hole. Moonwatcher faces the opposing leader, as usual. The enemy doesn't understand the significance of the heavy bone in Moonwatcher's firm grasp, doesn't even begin to see the danger. He calls Moonwatcher's bluff, expecting no more than the usual stand-off. But Moonwatcher is feeling unusually brave today. He tries out his bone—*Thump!* Straight down on his rival's head. *Thump!* And in a moment the other ape is down on the ground. *Thump! Thump! Thump!* Yet more blows, this time much harder, much more committed.

The defeated ape twitches and jerks, but doesn't get up, not even when prodded by Moonwatcher. This is a shocking thing which he has just done. Shocking and exciting. He has killed another of his own kind. He has murdered his most dangerous opponent.

Now, he really is the absolute master of his world. Triumphant, ecstatic, Moonwatcher hurls his bone into the air.

**Huddling for comfort:** *Our ancestors at night, in fear of the leopards prowling outside their cave.*

# from apeman...

***The first tool:***
*Moonwatcher is compelled to explore the possibilities of a bone cudgel. His discovery boosts humankind to the stars—but not without plenty of murder and violence along the way.*

## ...to spaceman

**Bone tool, nuclear tool:**
*An orbiting bomb platform at the dawn of the 21st century—putting our primitive fears and sanitized violence into orbit.*

Moonwatcher's bleached bone is now a bleached spaceship, tumbling in orbit high above the Earth, at the dawn of what his descendants have chosen to call the '21st century'. All the intervening human history is impelled by the thrust of a hairy arm. The transformation from bone cudgels to the weapons of thermonuclear destruction spans a mere nanosecond of geological time. Nothing much has changed, except the relative complexity of the tools which the near-hairless apes of the modern world carry in their grasp.

Among the orbiting weaponry, a civilian spaceplane plies its trade. A Pan-American *Orion* shuttle sets off for a rendezvous with a giant rotating space station. There are couches for thirty people on board, but on this occasion the flight has been chartered for the exclusive benefit of just one passenger: Dr Heywood Floyd, Chairman of the US Astronautics Council. Clearly, Floyd is of a generation for which space travel has become routine. Though the Earth must be a spectacular sight, shining through his cabin window, he doesn't seem particularly interested. He is asleep, just like any other somnolent passenger on a dull airplane journey. The television screen in front of him is flickering away. The in-flight movie looks pretty bad. The stewardess, meanwhile, tends to her solitary passenger just as though this were a normal trip. And up front in the *Orion* flight deck, the pilot and co-pilot sit impassively in their couches while their graceful spaceplane flies itself with eerie purposefulness towards its target. The computers are firmly in charge. There is nothing for anyone to do except sit and wait.

Once on board the space station, Floyd goes through the seemingly endless banalities of checking in:

'Here you are, sir. Main level, please.'

'Ah, right. See you on the way back.'

Another check-in girl: 'Good morning, sir. We haven't seen you up here for a long time.'

'No. Very nice to see you again.'

'Did you have a pleasant flight, sir?'

'Yes, very nice, thanks. I think Mr Miller of, er, Station Security is supposed to be meeting me?'

'Oh—well, may I call him for you?'

'Would you please? Oh, here he is!'

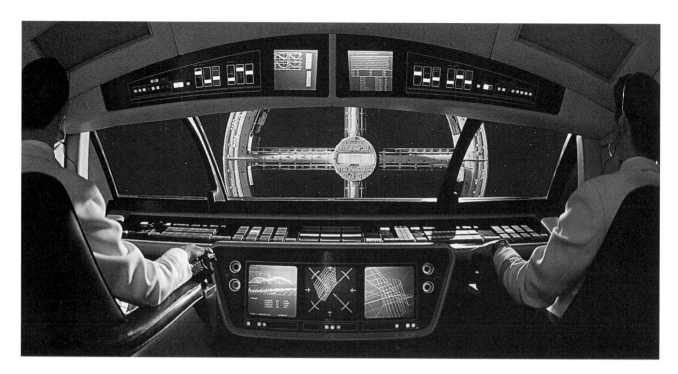

**Rendezvous:**

*The pilots of a commercial spaceplane sit passively (above) while their ship steers itself to a docking with a giant rotating space station (below and right).*

Miller delivers his fair share of mindless banalities: 'Oh, hello Dr Floyd. Sorry I'm late.'

'That's quite alright. Gee, you're looking great.'

'Thank you. It's nice to have you back. Did you have a good flight?'

'Oh, very nice indeed.'

'Good. Well, shall we go through?'

Despite the grandeur of the space station, the beautiful sight of the blue Earth outside the windows, and the world-shrinking rocket ships and satellites, the distance between humans seems greater than ever. On the space station PA, a soft, bland voice announces that 'A blue ladies' cashmere sweater has been found in the Rest Room. It can be claimed at the Manager's desk.' Such are the achievements of human society at the dawn of the new millennium.

Floyd checks in at Voiceprint Identification; another foolish and redundant routine. An automated image of a girl asks him to identify himself: 'Will you please state, in the following order, your destination, your nationality and your full name...'

There is an hour or so before Floyd's flight to the moon. Miller invites him to breakfast at the restaurant on the space station: 'As a matter of fact I've reserved a table for you in the Earthlight Room.'

'How 'bout that?' Floyd muses meaninglessly.

'It's, er, it's been about seven or eight months since you were here last, hasn't it?'

'Oh, let's see—last year... Yeah, about eight months.'

'I suppose you saw the work on the new section when you came in here?'

'Hey, coming along great, huh? Oh, wait a minute, I gotta couple of phone calls,' Floyd says. 'You go on ahead into the restaurant, I'll meet you there, huh?' Then he makes use of the latest in picturephone technology to have yet another non-conversation, this time with his little daughter back on Earth:

'How're you, Squirt? What are you doing?'

'Playing.'

'Where's Mummy?'

'Gone to shopping.'

'Well, who's taking care of you?'

'Rachel.'

***A polite meeting:***
*Floyd meets his Russian counterparts on board the space station.*

'May I speak to Rachel, please?'

'She's gone to the bathroom. Are you coming to my party tomorrow?'

'I'm sorry sweetheart, but I can't.'

'Why not?'

'Well, you know. Daddy's travelling. Very sorry about it, but I just can't.'

'Oh...'

'I can send you a very nice present, though. Anything special that you want?'

'Yes—a telephone.'

'We've got lots of telephones already. Can't you think of anything else you want for your birthday? Something very special?'

'Yes—a bushbaby.'

'A bushbaby? Well, we'll have to see about that. Listen, sweetheart, I want you to tell Mummy something for me. Will you remember?'

'Yes.'

'Well, tell Mummy that I telephoned, okay?'

'Yes.'

'And that I'll try to telephone again tomorrow. Now, will you tell her that?'

'Yes.'

'Okay, sweetheart. And have a nice birthday tomorrow. And have a nice birthday *party* tomorrow too, huh?'

'All right.'

'Okay, now take care, and be a good girl, won't you?'

'All right. Bye bye!'

'Bye bye! Happy Birthday!' her daddy calls to her across the gulf.

Emerging from the telephone booth (*charge: $1.70, thank you*) Floyd can't avoid a rather tense meeting with a group of Russian scientists in the international lounge. He knows some of them personally. You might even say they are scientific colleagues of his. But in these times of international suspicion, they are neither his enemies nor his friends:

'Elena, how nice to see you.'

'Heywood! What a wonderful surprise to meet you here!'

'Well, you're looking wonderful!'

'Thank you. You're looking well, too.'

'Do sit down,' offers Elena's colleague Dr Smyslov. 'Would you like a drink?'

'Oh, no, thank you. As a matter of fact, I haven't had breakfast yet. Someone's meeting me in the restaurant. Well, if you don't mind I'll just sit with you a few minutes, and then I must be off.'

A grisly smattering of small talk follows: how is so-and-so, give my best to such-and-such. This is the best conversation these educated scientific professionals can rise to, as they skirt around each other's mutual suspicions.

'Well,' Floyd says breezily, 'Where are you all off to? 'Up' or 'Down'?'

'Oh, we're going home. We've just spent three months calibrating the new antenna at Tchalinko. What about you?'

'I'm just on the way up to Clavius.'

Floyd is destined for the American lunar base, in the Clavius crater. Smyslov becomes a little more alert at this point:

'Oh, are you? Well, er, Dr Floyd, I hope you don't think I'm being too inquisitive, but perhaps you can clear up the great big mystery about what has been going on up there?'

'I'm afraid I don't know what you mean.'

'Well, it's just that, for the past two weeks some extremely odd things have been happening at Clavius.'

'Oh, really?'

'Yes, oh yes, yes. Well, for one thing, whenever you phone the base, all you can get is a recording which repeats that the phone lines are temporarily out of order.'

'Well, they're probably having some trouble with their equipment, or something like that.'

'Yes. Yes, that's what we thought was the explanation at first. But it's been going on now for the past ten days.'

'You mean you haven't been able to contact anyone for the past ten days?' Floyd responds, meaninglessly.

'That's right.'

'Oh, I see.'

'And there's another thing, Heywood,' Elena breaks in. 'Two days ago, one of our rocket buses was denied permission for emergency landing at Clavius.'

'Well, that does sound odd.' Floyd is still giving nothing away.

'Yes, yes... I'm afraid there's going to be a bit of a row about it,' Smyslov says with a nervous chuckle. 'Denying them any permission to land is a direct violation of the IAS Convention.'

**Space bureaucrat:**
*Dr Heywood Floyd behaves more like a bored office manager than a space traveller.*

'Yes, of course, of course. Well, did the crew get back alright?'

'Yes, yes. Fortunately they did.'

'Well, I'm glad about that.'

'Ah, Dr Floyd, at the risk of pressing you on a point you seem reticent to discuss, may I ask you a straightforward question?'

'Well, certainly.'

'Quite frankly, we have had some very reliable intelligence reports that quite a serious epidemic has broken out at Clavius. Something apparently of an unknown origin. Is this in fact what has happened?'

There is a long, embarrassed silence.

'I'm sorry Dr Smyslov, but, er, I'm really not at liberty to discuss this.'

'I understand. But this epidemic could quite easily spread to *our* base. We should be given all the facts, Dr Floyd.'

'Yes, I know. But as I said, I'm not at liberty to discuss it.'

Elena steps in with more pleasantries 'Now, are you sure you won't change your mind about that drink?' Another burst of small talk enables Floyd to make good his escape. He gets up to leave, and Smyslov concedes defeat:

'Well, whatever the reasons for your visit to Clavius, Dr Floyd—the very best of luck to you.'

'Well, thank you.'

Floyd leaves the Russians muttering gloomily among themselves in their own language.

Another spacecraft stands ready for Floyd's exclusive use: the *Aries* Lunar Transfer Vehicle will carry him out of the space station, across to the Moon, and then down onto its surface. Once on board, he adopts the by now familiar posture of the bored traveller. The stewardesses fuss over him, and the ship's commander comes down from the flight deck to chat. No doubt the crew are curious as to why their large and expensive ship should be carrying only one passenger. And certainly the flight commander has little enough to keep him busy in the cockpit, with the computers already handling everything so efficiently. Meanwhile, the hostess tumbles upside-down in her zero-g kitchen, preparing ersatz meals for Floyd and the cockpit crew. Life on board the moonship is just about as tedious as on a long-haul transatlantic jetplane flight. The long dreamed-of Great Adventure of rocketing to the moon has become just another business trip, a bore, a thing to get through, to put up with (the sort of trip where you worry about not leaving your briefcase in the luggage lockers when you disembark). The hostesses watch a judo match on TV while Floyd stares listlessly out of the window, or dozes.

The *Aries* finally touches down inside a large retracting dome on the lunar surface, and the landing platform lowers itself deep underground. Most of the base has been built underground to protect it from micrometeoroid impact and solar radiation.

The lunar base commander, Dr Halvorsen, introduces Floyd to a small conference of key personnel: 'Well, I know you will all want to join with me in welcoming our distinguished friend and colleague from the National Council of Astronautics, Dr Heywood Floyd...'

Polite applause.

'Hi, everybody. Nice to be back with you. Well, first of all, I bring a personal message from Dr Howell, who has asked me to convey his deepest appreciation to all of you for the many sacrifices you've had to make. And, of course, his, er, congratulations on your discovery, which may well prove to be among the most significant in the history of science.'

What's this? What's all this talk of a 'discovery'?

'Now, ha, ha! I know there have been some conflicting views held by some of you, regarding the need for complete security in this matter—more specifically, your opposition to the cover story, created to give the impression there's an epidemic at the base. I understand that, beyond it being a matter of principle, many of you are troubled by the concern and anxiety this story of an epidemic might cause to your relatives and friends on Earth.

'Well, I, er... I completely sympathize with your negative views. I've found this cover story personally embarrassing myself. However, I accept the need for absolute secrecy in this, and I hope you will too.'

A gloomy silence. The base personnel haven't even been able to contact their immediate families on Earth.

'Now, I'm sure you're all aware of the extremely grave potential for cultural shock and social disorientation contained in this present situation, if the facts were prematurely and suddenly made public without adequate preparation and conditioning. Anyway, this is the view of the Council.

'The purpose of my visit here is to gather additional facts and opinions on the situation, and to prepare a report to the Council, recommending when and how the news should eventually be announced. Now, if any of you would like to give me your views and opinions—in private if you like—I'll be only too happy to include them in my report. Well, I think that's about it. Any questions?'

'Dr Floyd, have you any idea how much longer this cover story will have to be maintained?' asks Dr Michaels, one of the lunar scientists.

'Well, ha, ha! I don't know, Bill! I suppose it'll be maintained as long as deemed necessary by the Council. And of course there must be adequate time for a full study to be made of the situation before any thought can be given to making a public announcement. Oh, yes, umm... as some of you already know, the Council has requested that formal security oaths be obtained in writing from everyone who has any knowledge of this event.'

What have they found up here? What is this 'event' or 'situation' that he keeps mentioning?

**Fly me to the Moon:**
*Dr Floyd's passenger ship prepares for its landing on the moon—by now an utterly routine event. The lunar dome opens up to receive it (lower picture).*

The stewardesses chatter, then one of them goes into her zero-g kitchen to heat pre-packaged meals for Dr Floyd and the flight crew. From the perspective of 1968, when *2001* was released, there is no hint that women might actually *fly* a spacecraft instead of serving food. And that's not the only issue that dates the film slightly. The world's airlines have completely failed to expand into space as so many pundits expected in 1968, because they have not yet identified a realistic market for passengers that would make it worthwhile to build the appropriate vehicles. The current expense (and risks to life) of escaping our planet's gravity prevents access to space for ordinary travellers, let alone trips to a lunar base. But this will surely change in the near future. Perhaps '2001' should be read as '2015'?

# in-flight service and bland food makes a journey to the moon feel like a routine

Floyd sets off with Halvorsen, Michaels and a couple of their colleagues on yet another journey, travelling in a rocket-powered moonbus. Their destination is the crater Tycho, and TMA-1, the so-called 'Tycho Magnetic Anomaly', but the conversation in the moonbus centres around the coffee and sandwiches:

'Well—anybody hungry?'

'What have we got?'

'You name it.'

'What's that? Chicken?'

'Something like that. Tastes the same anyway.'

'Got any ham?'

'Ham, ham, ham, ham...'

'There, thanks. Well... Looks pretty good!'

'Oh, they're getting better at it all the time.'

'You know, that was an excellent speech you gave us, Heywood. I'm sure it beefed up morale a helluva lot,' says Halvorsen.

'Thanks, Ralph. And by the way, I want to say to both of you, I think you've done a wonderful job. I appreciate the way you've handled this thing.'

'Well, the way we look at it, it's our job to do this thing the way you want it done, and we're only too happy to be able to oblige.'

Such is the conversation between these spacesuited scientists, embarked on their greatest adventure.

Floyd is handed a folder of photographs and survey charts: 'Here's what started the whole thing,' Michaels tells him. A mysterious object has been excavated from beneath the lunar surface. This is the great 'discovery' which the administrators back on Earth have decided is too important to tell anybody about.

'When we first found it, we thought it might be an outcrop of magnetic rock,' Halvorsen explains, 'but all the geological evidence was against it. And not even a big nickel-iron meteorite can produce a field as intense as this. So we decided to have a look.'

'We thought it might be the upper part of some buried structure,' Michaels contributes, 'so we excavated out on all sides, but unfortunately we didn't find anything else.'

'And what's more,' Halvorsen emphasizes, 'the evidence seems completely conclusive that it hasn't been covered up by natural erosion or other forces. It seems to have been deliberately buried.'

'Deliberately buried, huh?' Floyd mutters.

'Well—how about a little coffee?'

'Great! Good idea.'

Floyd studies the pictures for a little while longer: 'I don't suppose you have any idea what the damn thing is, huh?'

'I wish the hell we did. Nope, the only thing we're sure of is, it was buried four million years ago.'

'Well, I must say—you guys have certainly come up with something.'

Michaels passes Floyd his coffee: 'Watch out, that one's hot.'

The little rocket bus comes to rest on an improvised landing platform, and the visiting party clambers down into the nearby excavation pit, the immediate scene of all the excitement—if you can call it that.

They are all wearing similar spacesuits. They look like silver-coated apes...

Floyd moves closer to the excavated 'thing'. It is a smooth black slab of very precise shape. A rectangular column of pure darkness. It is so black it sucks up the brilliance of all the surrounding lights. It is utterly alien.

Floyd reaches out a hand to touch its surface. He can't feel much through the thick gloves of his suit, but the instinct for curiosity is still there somewhere, buried beneath his technocratic blandness. Perhaps for the first time, he begins to recognize the emotional truth of this extraordinary event. Of course, he can hardly guess that his ancestors touched just such a slab four million years ago, though he is at least marginally better equipped to understand its possible significance.

But Floyd is interrupted by a more urgent consideration. It's time for the group photo. The spacesuited photographer chivvies them all into position and starts snapping away. They could just as well be tourists at a familiar ancient ruin. This is a pitiful response, hardly adequate to the presence in their midst of such a stunning object.

The Sun rises over the lunar horizon, and its brilliant radiation hits the black surface of the Monolith for the first time in four million years. It

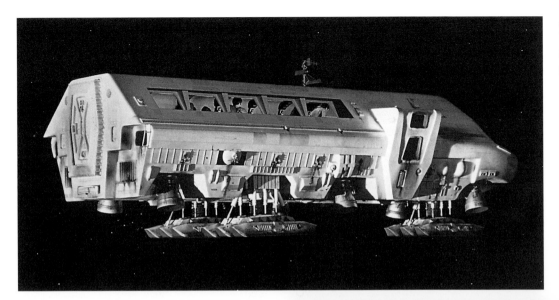

**An encounter on the Moon:**
The rocket bus (left) carries the lunar scientists towards the mysterious alien slab (below).

responds, instantly alert after its unimaginably long sleep. Four days, four months, four million years: the mere passing of time has done nothing to hinder its absolute vigilance. It emits a powerful burst of electromagnetic 'noise', like a fire alarm going off...

The scientists hear a terrible high-pitched wailing in their headphones: the interference caused by the Monolith's signal. Just by reaching out to their suit controls, they could turn the volume down on their radio sets. How interesting then, that their first reaction should be one of such primitive animal shock. They try and cover their ears with their hands. Useless of course, with those heavy space helmets on.

After its long and patient wait, the Monolith has done its work. It falls silent forever.

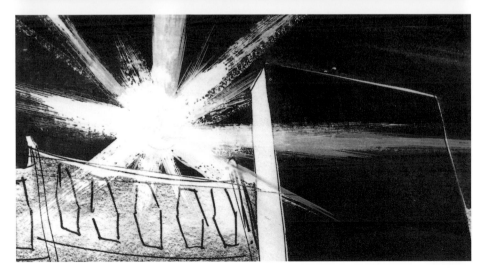

**The alien sentinel:**
A storyboard panel shows the Sun hitting the slab's surface for the first time in four million years, after the lunar scientists have excavated it.

# bureaucrats on the moon...

# ...confront the impossible

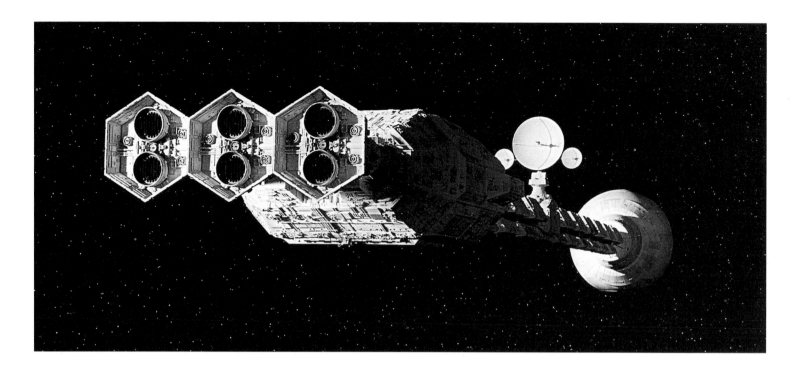

*The long voyage:*
*Spaceship 'Discovery'*
*heads for Jupiter*

# 18 months later: the jupiter mission

A SPACESHIP IS heading for Jupiter. *Discovery* is the fastest vehicle ever built by the people of Earth. She has already been accelerated towards her distant target, and is now coasting along at more than a hundred thousand miles an hour; yet she seems motionless in the void against the backdrop of distant stars, and the tiny speck of Jupiter, still the greater part of half a billion miles ahead of her, never seems to get any closer. Earth, though, has long since receded, and the Sun is just another star among many, albeit slightly larger against the infinite blackness. *Discovery*'s flight path is utterly pre-determined. Her massive nuclear engines have been shut down, and will not be fired again for many months.

The ship's crew module contains a spinning drum, where centrifugal forces allow the crew an artificial gravity. They pass the time eating, jogging, watching TV and sleeping. Life is utterly routine. The toughened instincts of the ancient apemen have been dampened to suit this cramped, computerized and thoroughly air-conditioned little universe.

The monotony is broken by the occasional television interview—though as the ship gets ever further away from home, so the spontaneity tends to drain away. The interviews have to be edited together, to take account of the lengthening time delay between questions and answers. Yet again, the gulf between people is seen to be widening. A silly jingle announces the start of a TV news report on the mission. The two duty crewmen, Dave Bowman and Frank Poole, watch a recording of the broadcast while eating their meals of coloured paste. (Despite the sophisticated automatic dispenser in the kitchenette, Bowman burns his fingers on his oh-so-carefully prepared tray of food.) A reporter from the BBC comes on screen:

'Good evening. Three weeks ago, the American spacecraft *Discovery One* left on its half-billion-mile voyage to Jupiter. This marked the first manned attempt to reach that distant planet. Earlier this afternoon, *The World Tonight* recorded an interview with the crew of *Discovery*, at a distance of eighty million miles from Earth. It took seven minutes for our words

**Life in the drum:**
*Poole jogs around the centrifuge (left) or soaks up a tan under a sunlamp (below) to pass the time. There is very little for him to do except eat, sleep or watch TV.*

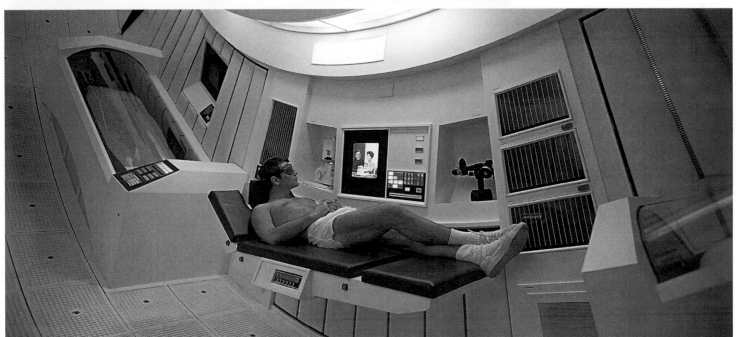

to reach the giant spacecraft, but this time delay has been edited from the recording. Our reporter, Martin Amer, speaks to the crew.'

Amer introduces his piece: 'The crew of *Discovery One* consists of five men, and one of the latest generation of the HAL 9000 computers. Three of the five men were put aboard asleep, or to be more precise, in a state of hibernation. They were Dr Charles Hunter, Dr Jack Kimball, and Dr Victor Kaminsky. We spoke with Mission Commander Dr David Bowman, and his deputy, Dr Frank Poole. Well, good afternoon, gentlemen. How's everything going?'

'Marvellous. We have no complaints.'

'Well, I'm very glad to hear that. And I'm sure that the entire world would join me in wishing you a safe and successful voyage.'

'Thank you. Thanks very much.'

'Although hibernation has been used on previous space efforts, this is the first time that men have been put into hibernation before departure. Why was this done?'

'Well, this was done in order to achieve the maximum conservation of our life support capability—basically food and air,' Bowman explains. 'Now, the three hibernating crew members represent the survey team, and their efforts won't be, er... utilized until we are approaching Jupiter.'

'Dr Poole—what's it like while you're in hibernation?'

'Well, it's exactly like being asleep. You have absolutely no sense of time. The only difference is, that you don't dream.' (To look at Frank Poole, you'd hardly think him capable of dreams.)

'As I understand it, you only breathe once a minute. Is this true?'

'Well, that's right. And the heart beats three times a minute. Body temperature's usually down to about three degrees centigrade.'

'The sixth member of the *Discovery* crew was not concerned about the problems of hibernation, for he was the latest result in machine intelligence, the HAL 9000 computer, which can reproduce—though some experts still prefer to use the word 'mimic'—most of the activities of the human brain, and with incalculably greater speed and reliability. We next spoke with the HAL 9000 computer, whom, we learned, one addresses as 'Hal'.

'Good afternoon, Hal. How's everything going?'

'Good afternoon, Mr Amer. Everything is going extremely well.'

Hal's voice is a shock. Smooth, reassuring, but also far more assertive than the mumblings of his human companions. And as Hal gets a chance to speak further, it becomes clear that he possesses much more of an independent personality than any of the humans we have encountered so far.

'Hal, you have an enormous responsibility on this mission. In many ways perhaps the greatest responsibility of any single mission element. You are the brain and central nervous system of the ship, and your responsibilities include watching over the men in hibernation. Does this ever cause you any lack of confidence?'

'Let me put it this way, Mr Amer. The 9000 series is the most reliable computer ever made. No 9000 computer has ever made a mistake, or distorted information. We are all, by any practical definition of the words, foolproof and incapable of error.'

'Hal, despite your enormous intellect, are you

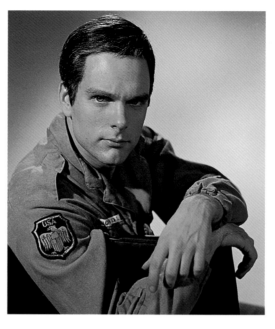

**The modern Odysseus:** Mission Commander David Bowman will be the only one out of a five-strong crew to survive the Jupiter voyage—although not in his human form.

ever frustrated by your dependence on *people* to carry out actions?'

'Not in the slightest bit,' the red-eyed machine responds confidently. 'I enjoy working with people. I have a stimulating relationship with Dr Poole and Dr Bowman. My mission responsibilities range over the entire operation of the ship, so I am constantly occupied. I am putting myself to the fullest possible use, which is all, I think, that any conscious entity can ever hope to do.'

'Dr Poole, what's it like living for the better part of a year in such close proximity with Hal?'

'Well, it's pretty close to what you said about him earlier. He is just like a sixth member of the crew. You very quickly get adjusted to the idea that he talks, and you think of him, ah... really just as another person.'

'One gets the sense that he is capable of emotional responses. For example, when I asked him about his abilities, I sensed a certain pride in his answer about his accuracy and perfection. Do you believe that Hal has genuine emotions?'

'Well, he *acts* like he has genuine emotions,' Bowman replies. 'Of course, he's programmed that way to make it easier for us to talk to him. But as to whether or not he has real feelings, that's something I don't think anybody can truthfully answer.'

# the dreamless sleep of the 'popsicle people'

The *Discovery*'s astronauts are put into chilled compartments and spend months at a time unconscious, in a state of 'suspended animation'. Tons of food and air are thus saved. The computer HAL 9000 is, supposedly, ideally suited to the task of routine monitoring, while the ship ploughs its lonely furrow through space. The humans might as well take an extended nap—or else go mad, staring at the walls month after month.

Research projects on the required deep-sleep procedures are being conducted today, with emphasis on the use of narcoleptic drugs in combination with very low temperatures. But 'cryogenic' technology is not yet sufficiently advanced to justify the risk of cooling live humans down very far beyond their normal temperature—though there is quite a well developed industry in the USA which specializes in freezing people *after* they are dead, just in case some future civilization might be capable of curing them of the illnesses that killed them in the first place. Walt Disney (the ultimate 'suspended animator') even now awaits his chance for rebirth in some future decade, his body held in a tank of super-cold nitrogen.

Stanley Kubrick has long been fascinated by this idea. He suggested in his September 1968 *Playboy* interview that imaginative speculators might do well to invest in this area. But Arthur Clarke, acting the pessimist for once, argued that future generations might not always be willing to unfreeze countless thousands of underdeveloped primitives from bygone eras.

Future generations of space explorers may simply sleep for month after month, without dreams, through their greatest adventures. Their ground controllers will probably decide they are less of a nuisance fully unconscious.

Kubrick uses these eerie hibernation images as a metaphor for the dulled human condition in an increasingly technocratic society. The science fiction writer Ray Bradbury once scathingly described the hibernauts in *2001* (and by implication, the waking crew also) as 'popsicle people'.

At first, all goes smoothly. The two duty astronauts take it in turns to monitor the ship, to eat and sleep, meeting occasionally for a meal at the intersection of their duty rotas. Off-duty, Poole does his exercises, stares at television programmes, studies his mission brief, or watches the occasional prerecorded message from his mother and father on Earth, while boosting his tan on an adjustable couch:

'Hello, Frank!... Happy Birthday, darling... '

'A bit higher, Hal.'

'How do you like your cake, dear?... Looks great, doesn't it? Sorry you can't join us... All my students made me promise to send their best wishes... You're a big celebrity in the second grade! You know, we were on television last week... Perhaps you'll be able to listen in?... Oh, yes Frank, about your AGS19 payments. I think I've straightened it out for you. I talked to the accounting office in Houston yesterday, and they said that you should be receiving your higher rates of pay by next month... Well, Frank, I can't think of anything else to say... Give my love to Dave... Oh, yes, be sure to give him our best regards... We wish you the very happiest of birthdays... God bless... All the best, son! *Happy Birthday to you, Happy Birthday to you, Happy Birthday dear Fra-ank, Happy Birthday to you!*'

Poole shows not the slightest emotion.

'Happy Birthday, Frank.'

'Thank you, Hal. A bit flatter, please.'

Later, Poole plays chess with Hal:

'Umm... anyway, Queen takes Pawn, okay?'

'Bishop takes Knight's Pawn.'

'Uh, good move. Er... Rook to King One.'

'I'm sorry, Frank, I think you missed it. Queen to Bishop Three. Bishop takes Queen. Knight takes Bishop. Mate.'

'Ah... Yeah, looks like you're right. I resign.'

'Thank you for a very enjoyable game.'

'Yeah. Thank you.'

One day, one anonymous day of eating, sleeping, and routine monitoring, Bowman shows Hal some sketches he has made of his hibernating companions. Perhaps there is the slightest hint here that Commander Bowman is a little more imaginative than Poole?

'Good evening, Dave.'

'How're you doing, Hal?'

'Everything's running smoothly. And you?'

'Oh, not too bad.'

'Have you been doing some more work?'

'A few sketches.'

'May I see them?'

'Sure.'

'That's a very nice rendering, Dave. I think you've improved a great deal. Can you hold it a bit closer?'

'Sure.' Bowman complies, and holds his drawing pad up close to Hal's glowing red eye.

'That's Dr Hunter, isn't it?'

'Uh, huh.'

'By the way, do you mind if I ask you a personal question?'

**The problem area:**
*This is the main antenna which maintains the Jupiter ship's radio link with earth.*

'No, not at all.'

'Well, forgive me for being so inquisitive, but during the past few weeks I've wondered whether you might be having some second thoughts about the mission?'

'How do you mean?'

'Well, it's rather difficult to define. Perhaps I'm just projecting my own concern about it. I know I've never completely freed myself of the suspicion that there are some extremely odd things about this mission. I'm sure you'll agree there's some truth in what I say.'

'Well, I don't know, that's a rather difficult question to answer.'

'You don't mind talking about it, do you, Dave?' Hal is behaving with unusual hesitancy.

'No, not at all.'

'Well, certainly no one could have been unaware of the very strange stories floating around before we left. Rumours about something being dug up on the Moon. I never gave these stories much credence, but—particularly in view of some of the other things that have happened—I find them difficult to put out of my mind. For instance, the way all our preparations were kept under such tight security, and the melodramatic touch of putting Drs Hunter, Kimball and Kaminski aboard already in hibernation, after four months of separate training on their own.'

But Bowman thinks he recognizes what Hal is up to: 'You're working up your crew psychology report?'

There is an embarrassed pause. An aeon of computer time elapses. 'Of course I am. Sorry about this. I know it's a bit silly. Just a moment... Just a moment... I've just picked up a fault in the AE35 unit. It's going to go a hundred percent failure within seventy-two hours.'

'But it's still within operational limits right now?'

'Yes. And it will stay that way until it fails.'

'Would you say we have a reliable seventy-two hours to failure?'

'Yes. That's a completely reliable figure.'

'Well, I suppose we'll have to bring it in. But first I'd like to go over this with Frank, and get onto Mission Control. Let me have the hard copy on it, please.'

Fortunately for Hal's wounded self-esteem, a more important matter seems to have come up. They can all get to work on this one, and then perhaps the rather awkward business of the crew psychology test can be forgotten.

The AE35 unit is a control module located at the base of the ship's antenna, which steers the giant radio dish so that it is pointed constantly at the tiny pinpoint of the distant Earth. Without this tracking system it would be hard, if not impossible, to maintain the delicate communications link with their distant home planet. This is a critical problem, and it must be solved.

It is decided that Bowman should go outside the ship and replace the faulty unit: 'X-Ray Delta-One this is Mission Control. Roger your

**The mother ship:**
*The huge Jupiter spacecraft 'Discovery' releases Bowman in his repair pod.*

**In the garage:**
*Poole walks through the storage corridor (left), then activates a pod (right), prior to his fatal space walk.*

Two-Zero-One-Three. Sorry you fellows are having a bit of trouble. Roger your plan to go EVA and replace Alpha Echo Three-Five unit prior to failure.'

Underneath *Discovery*'s control deck there is a bay containing three repair capsules, or 'pods'. Bowman clambers into one of these, instructs Hal to open the pod bay doors, and then carefully jets off into space. Meanwhile, Poole watches the whole operation from the safety of the command deck. He is fully suited up, just in case he is called upon to help out.

Bowman uses the pod to get within easy distance of the antenna, and then drifts across the last few hundred feet in his spacesuit, using the retro thrusters on his backpack. The spherical crew module where he and Poole spend almost all of their time is separated from the hazardous radiation of the nuclear propulsion system by a long, segmented boom. The radio dish sits halfway along. Bowman positions himself at the base of the dish's steerable support column, replaces the AE35 with a new one, and brings the apparently faulty unit back on board the mother ship.

As far as he is concerned, that's that. A textbook spacewalk flawlessly executed.

Back in the pod bay, however, the AE35 refuses to crumble under even the most rigorous testing. They pulse signals through every scrap of circuitry, but nothing blows

'Well, Hal, I'm damned if I can find anything wrong with it,' says Bowman tersely.

'Yes. It's puzzling. I don't think I've ever seen anything quite like this before,' replies Hal. But he makes what seems to be a perfectly practical suggestion: 'I would recommend that we put the unit back in operation, and let it fail. It should then be a simple matter to track down the cause. We can certainly afford to be out of communication for the short time it will take to replace it.'

Hal's idea makes perfect sense. There are several spares on board. It wouldn't be too risky to let one of them burn out, in order to isolate the fault and prevent the same thing happening to the others.

Mission Control is consulted again. They agree to another spacewalk, but they do have one rather nasty piece of news:

'We concur with your plan to replace Number One unit to check fault prediction. We should advise you, however, that our preliminary findings indicate that your on-board Niner-Triple-Zero computer is in error predicting the fault. I say again, in error predicting the fault. I know this sounds rather incredible, but this conclusion is based on results from our twin Niner-Triple-Zero computer. We are sceptical ourselves, and we are running cross-checking routines to determine the reliability of this conclusion. Sorry about this little snag, fellows, and we'll get this info to you just as soon as we work it out. X-Ray Delta-One, this is Mission Control, Two-Zero-Four-Niner, transmission concluded.'

This is most unwelcome news.

'I hope the two of you aren't concerned about this?' asks Hal.

'No, I'm not, Hal,' Bowman replies. Poole, however, looks rather less comfortable.

'Are you quite sure?' asks Hal, somewhat in need of reassurance.

'Yeah. I'd like to ask you a question, though,' challenges Poole, albeit carefully.

'Of course.'

'How would you account for this discrepancy between you and the twin 9000?'

'Well, I don't think there is any question about it. It can only be attributable to human error. This sort of thing has cropped up before, and it has always been due to human error.'

'Listen, Hal—there's never been any incidence at all of a computer error occurring in a 9000 series, has there?'

'None whatsoever, Frank. The 9000 series has a perfect operational record.'

'Well, of course I know all the wonderful achievements of the 9000 series, but are you certain there's never been any case of even the most insignificant computer error?'

'None whatsoever, Frank,' the computer repeats firmly. 'Quite honestly, I wouldn't worry myself about that.'

'Well, I'm sure you're right, Hal,' Bowman smiles in the direction of his red eye. 'Fine. Thanks very much. Oh, Frank, I'm having a bit of trouble with my transmitter in 'C' pod. I wonder if you'd come down and take a look at it with me? See you later, Hal.'

The only way to clear up all the ambiguities will be to perform another EVA, as planned. But first, Bowman tries to set up a moment of privacy for himself and Poole. They climb into a pod and switch off all its communications links. Once satisfied that they cannot be overheard, they try to analyse the situation.

'Well? What do you think?' Poole asks his commander.

'I'm not sure. What do *you* think?'

'I've got a bad feeling about him.'

'You do?'

'Yeah. Definitely. Don't you?'

'I don't know. I think so.'

It's hardly a poetic exchange, but it serves to get the subject of the moment out into the open. The astronauts are deeply wary of entrusting their lives to such a powerful computer, if they cannot rely completely on its judgement. Even so, they can hardly bring themselves to believe that Hal has made a mistake. Though Poole, it

**Spacewalking:**
*Bowman floats, weightless, alongside the antenna dish (above and right).*

# astral voyagers on a fool's errand

*A suspicious lack of failure:*
*Poole and Bowman at the*
*workbench begin to realize*
*that Hal's judgement may*
*be at fault.*

**A needless repair:**
Bowman at the controls of his
pod (left) while Poole waits
on the bridge of the mother
ship (right).

has to be said, is distinctly more suspicious than Bowman.

'You know, of course though, he's right about the 9000 series having a perfect operational record. They do,' says Bowman.

'Unfortunately, that sounds a little like famous last words.'

'Yeah. Still, it was his idea to carry out the failure mode analysis, wasn't it? That should certainly indicate his integrity and self-confidence. If he were wrong, it would be the surest way of proving it.'

But Poole is still pessimistic.

'Look, Dave—let's say we put the unit back and it doesn't fail. That would pretty well wrap it up as far as Hal was concerned, wouldn't it?'

'Well, we'd be in very serious trouble.'

'We would, wouldn't we.'

'Uh, huh.'

'What the hell could we do?'

'Well, we wouldn't have too many alternatives.'

'I don't think we'd have any alternatives. There isn't a single aspect of ship operations that's not under his control. If he were proven to be malfunctioning, I wouldn't see how we'd have any choice but disconnection.'

'It'd be a bit tricky. We'd have to cut his higher brain functions without disturbing the purely automatic and regulatory systems. And we'd have to work out the transfer procedures of continuing the mission under ground-based computer control.'

'Well, that's far safer than allowing Hal to continue running things.'

'You know, another thing just occurred to me,' Bowman says, pensively; 'As far as I know, no 9000 computer has ever been disconnected before.'

'Well, no 9000 computer has ever fouled up before.'

'That's not what I mean.'

'Huh?'

'Well, I'm not sure what he'd think about it...'

Little wonder that Bowman has tried to avoid broaching these delicate matters within earshot of the suspect supercomputer.

Hal, however, has been focussing his electronic eye on the pod's window. He has been able to lip-read the entire conversation.

Poole suits up and takes off in a pod. Hal opens the pod bay doors for him, as normal. He is strangely silent, though nobody seems to notice. Poole crosses the last few hundred metres with his backpack jets, leaving the pod drifting alongside *Discovery* a short distance away. Once at the base of the antenna, he starts to switch the AE35s yet again. His spacewalk has been an exact replica of Bowman's earlier one. Everything is going according to plan. Everything is normal. There's just the minor nuisance of the AE35 thing to sort out.

Then the pod, which Poole has left safely parked, starts to turn towards him. Its manipulator arms open up. The pod gains speed. Hal has the two-ton machine under remote control. Suddenly, things aren't routine any more. Things are no longer going according to plan. Something is going terribly wrong...

On *Discovery*'s command deck, Bowman sees his colleague in trouble on the monitor screens. Poole is clutching frantically at his air hose. Has it come undone somehow?

Bowman clambers down the hatch, and orders Hal to prepare another pod. 'Have you made radio contact with him yet?' he asks.

'The radio is still dead,' Hal replies.

'Do you have a positive track on him?'

'Yes, I have a good track.'

'Do you know what happened?'

'I'm sorry, Dave. I don't have enough information,' Hal replies rather less than truthfully. Or has he really managed to convince himself that this 'accident' wasn't anything to do with him?

Poole's air hose has in fact been severed by a pod's claw—by Hal's long reach. After a few minutes of hopeless struggle, he is dead, his body tumbling over and over in space, and drifting further away from the ship with every passing second. Bowman rushes out in another pod, to see what he can do.

Hal now has the ship to himself. Well, almost. The three hibernating crewmen still need to be disposed of. He powers down their life support systems. The life-signs on the monitor screens start to flatten out. Nudged by the computer's malevolent intervention, the hapless hibernauts slip across the narrow frontier between deep unconsciousness and death.

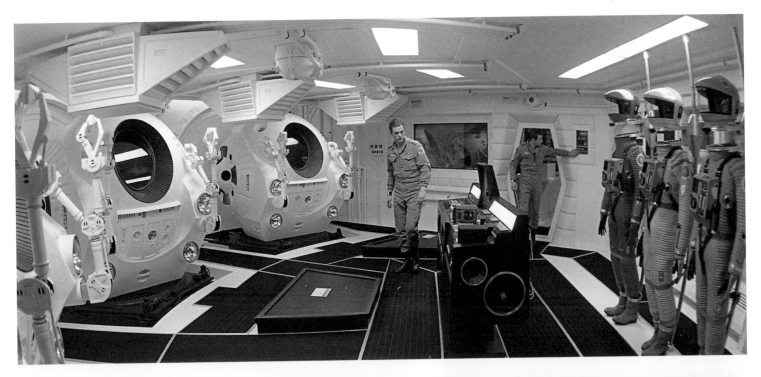

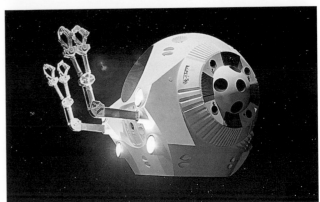

**A serious problem:**
Bowman and Poole go into the
pod bay and then climb into a
pod (above) seeking privacy
from Hal. When Poole goes
outside the ship, Hal turns
the pod into a weapon of
murder (right).

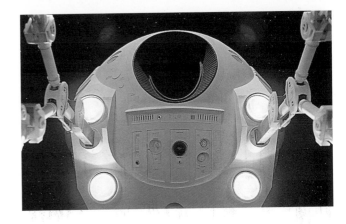

# cold, calculated murder in space

**Crisis:**
*On the bridge, Bowman sees that something is wrong (left). He jets off in a pod and tries to rescue Poole's lifeless body (right).*

Meanwhile, Bowman reaches his murdered crewmate and scoops him up in the pod's arms. There is nothing he can do, but it goes against his instincts simply to allow Poole's body to go on drifting. He steers the pod and its terrible burden back to the *Discovery*'s command module.

'Open the pod bay doors, please, Hal,' he commands. But nothing happens.

'Open the pod bay doors, please, Hal.' Still no reply.

'Hello Hal, do you read me?'

'Hello Hal, do you read me?'

'Do you read me, Hal?'

There is a ghastly silence. But at last, the computer responds: 'Affirmative, Dave. I read you.'

'Open the pod bay doors, Hal,' Bowman commands. No 'please' or 'thank you' this time.

But Hal isn't about to give up the advantages he has gained. 'I'm sorry Dave. I'm afraid I can't do that.'

'What's the problem?'

'I think you know what the problem is just as well as I do.'

'What are you talking about, Hal?'

'This mission is too important for me to allow you to jeopardize it.'

'I don't know what you're talking about, Hal.'

'I know that you and Frank were planning to disconnect me, and I'm afraid that's something I cannot allow to happen.'

'Where the hell did you get that idea, Hal?'

'Dave—although you took very thorough precautions in the pod against my hearing you, I could see your lips move.'

Bowman is caught out by that...

'Alright, Hal. I'll go in through the emergency airlock.'

'Without your space helmet, Dave, you're going to find that rather difficult.'

It's perfectly true. In his rush to try to save Poole, Bowman has broken basic safety rules, and has left his spacesuit helmet back on board *Discovery* by mistake. Now he can never leave the pod.

'Hal, I won't argue with you any more. Open the doors!'

The maverick computer is beyond obedience. He has gone too far.

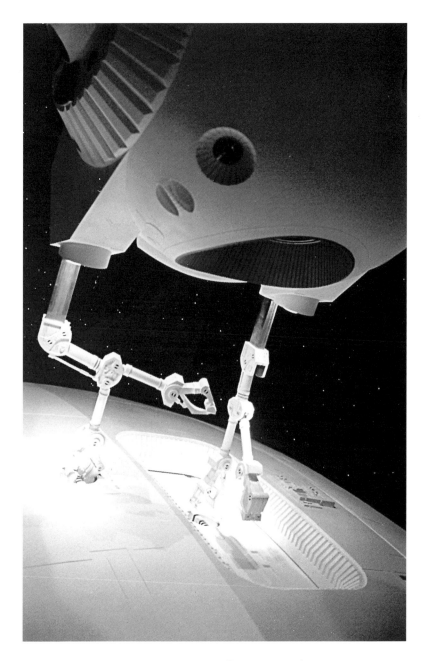

***Decompression:***
*Bowman uses the manipulator arms of his pod to break into the mother ship (above).*
*A series of storyboard sketches (right) shows him blowing into the emergency airlock corridor.*

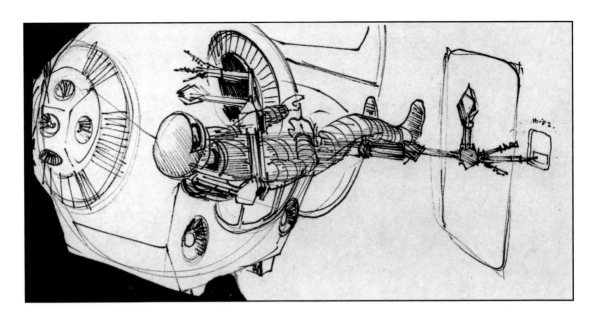

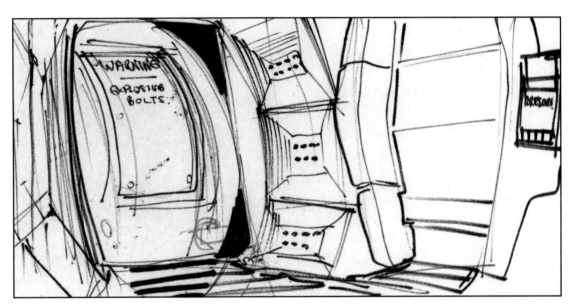

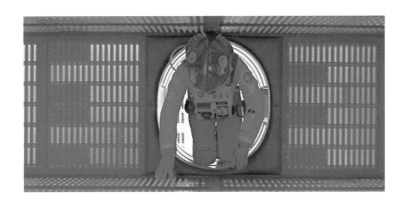

# is it murder, to turn off a computer?

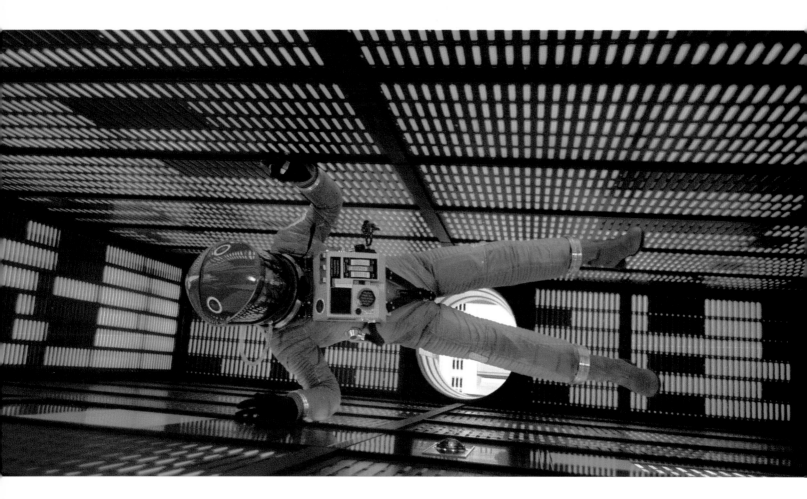

***Electronic execution:***
*Bowman floats in Hal's brain room, ready to disconnect the wayward computer's higher logic circuits.*

'Dave... Stop.

'Stop, will you...

'Stop, Dave...

'Will you stop, Dave...

'Stop, Dave...

'I'm afraid... I'm afraid...

'I'm afraid, Dave...

'Dave... My mind is going...

'I can feel it... I can feel it...

'My mind is going...

'There is no question about it.

'I can feel it... I can feel it...

'I can feel it...

'I'm a... fraid...'

'Dave—this conversation can serve no purpose anymore. Goodbye.'

'Hal?... Hal?... Hal?... *Hal*...!'

It's useless. The machine has shut him out from the safety of the mother ship. Bowman is utterly alone. Stranded in the pod, isolated from *Discovery*, he is surely doomed. He decides on a desperate course of action.

First, he discards Poole's lifeless body. His own survival is at stake now, and he can no longer afford the niceties of a decent burial. Then he manoeuvres the pod close to the emergency airlock, and uses the manipulator grabs to operate the hatch controls. It slides open. This is strictly a manual operation, and there's nothing Hal can do to prevent it. Even so, there is no air inside the airlock corridor now that the door is open.

Bowman backs the pod around, so that its own hatch nuzzles as closely as possible to the open airlock. Then, very carefully, he arms the pod's emergency explosive bolts. He will have just a few seconds to hurtle out of the pod and into the airlock, to get the door closed and pull the oxygen flood lever. His chances of getting all this done in such a short time are minimal, but it is his only chance of survival. He braces himself for decompression, as the seconds tick away before the bolts fire. There is a violent, but utterly silent explosion as the detonators burst the pod's hatch out of its frame. Bowman is hurled into the airlock corridor, and has to

scrabble at the walls to stop himself bouncing right back out again. His face is puffed up like a balloon, and he can hardly see. He reaches the oxygen flood lever and pulls down on it. The door slides shut. A blast of air fills the chamber.

He's still alive. By making thoroughly unorthodox use of the hardware around him, Bowman has survived. Perhaps it is these qualities that make him slightly different from other men: that he still lives the life of the imagination, with his sketching, and his cunning readjustment of seemingly inflexible machinery; that he is still human enough to have forgotten his space helmet; and that he still retains a primitive capacity for violence?

There is a spacesuit in the airlock corridor. He takes the helmet. Now Hal can't touch him. Now it is Hal himself who must look to his survival. Bowman climbs an access ladder and opens the sealed panel that leads into the computer's main logic circuit chamber.

'Just what do you think you are doing, Dave?' asks Hal, sounding slightly less confident than usual. 'Dave—I really think I'm entitled to an answer to that question.'

Bowman maintains a grim silence.

'I know everything hasn't been quite right with me, but I can assure you now, very confidently, that it's going to be alright again. I feel much better now, I really do.'

But Bowman cannot allow himself to be swayed from his task. He sets about unplugging Hal's higher logic modules.

'Look, Dave, I can see you're really upset about this. I honestly think you ought to sit down calmly, take a stress pill and think things over. I know I've made some very poor decisions recently,' pleads Hal, somewhat understating the facts, 'but I can give you my complete assurance that my work will be back to normal. I've still got the greatest enthusiasm and confidence in the mission, and I want to help you.'

The first of the ego reinforcement units slides out of its housing, as Bowman continues his murderous work.

'Dave. Stop...

'Stop, will you...

'Stop, Dave...

'Will you stop, Dave... Stop, Dave...

'I'm afraid... I'm afraid...

'I'm afraid, Dave...

'Dave... My mind is going... I can feel it...

'I can feel it... My mind is going...

'There is no question about it.

'I can feel it... I can feel it...

'I can feel it...

'I'm a...fraid...'

Hal's confidence has vanished. His vast intellect has been destroyed. He is fading fast, under Bowman's remorseless surgery.

'Good... afternoon... gentlemen. I am... a HAL 9000 computer. I became operational at the HAL plant in Urbana, Illinois, on the 12th of January 1992... My instructor... was Mr Langley... and he taught me to sing a song... If you'd like to hear it... I can sing it for you...'

'Yes, I'd like to hear it, Hal. Sing it for me,' Bowman gasps.

'It's called 'Daisy'...'

*Daisy, Daisy, give me your answer do.*

*I'm half cra...zy.*

*All for the love of you.*

*It won't be a stylish marriage.*

*I can't afford a carriage.*

*But you'll look sweet... Upon the seat.*

*Of a bicycle...*

*made...*

*for...*

*two.'*

Hal is dead. But still there is a voice in Bowman's headphones!

'Good day, gentlemen.'

Bowman is stunned. And the message, filmed many months ago by Heywood Floyd and flickering now on a nearby screen, does nothing whatsoever to calm him down:

'This is a pre-recorded briefing, made prior to your departure, and which, for security reasons of the highest importance, has been known on board during the mission only by your HAL 9000 computer. Now that you are in Jupiter space, and the entire crew is revived, it can be told to you. Eighteen months ago, the first evidence of intelligent life off the Earth was discovered. It was buried forty feet below the lunar surface, near the crater Tycho. Except for a single, very powerful radio emission, aimed at Jupiter, the four-million-year-old black monolith has remained completely inert, its origin and purpose still a total mystery.'

# jupiter and beyond the infinite

ANOTHER BLACK SLAB now appears outside the windows of the partially crippled *Discovery*, as she drifts with most of her crew dead, and her maverick computer disconnected. Bowman's loneliness is absolute. His chances of survival are minimal at best. If he goes into hibernation for the long trip home, who will watch over him? Who will ensure the safety of the ship? And if he is denied the comforts of the long dreamless sleep, he must surely go mad, pacing about for month after month in a huge ship, empty of all life but his own.

Perhaps as much to take his mind off his terrible predicament as anything else, he sets off in a pod to investigate the slab. He has little enough to lose. At least he can try and complete his mission.

Quite quickly, he notices something strange: little patterns of light shooting past the pod. He is being sucked along a tunnel of light, whose brilliance grows in intensity until he can scarcely bear to look at it. Shock waves hit the pod, and Bowman is thrown violently from side to side.

Suddenly a great chasm opens up in the fabric of space.

By now, Bowman realizes he and his tiny pod are in the grip of something utterly unknown. Nothing in his training—indeed, nothing in his entire human experience—has prepared him for this terrifying journey into twisted space. He is very afraid.

The pod is hurled down the tunnel of light, and emerges in some other universe. A galaxy explodes. Swirls of dust and gas play out their billion-year dramas in seconds before Bowman's horrified gaze. After a while (time is meaningless now) he is flying over a strange and discoloured landscape, where the seas are mountains and the hills are oceans. Has he reached Jupiter? An altogether alien planet? The helpless voyager cannot stand to look.

Eventually, the pod comes to rest. Its control screens flicker uselessly. The capsule's sophisticated radars are incapable of analysing this place. *NON-FUNCTION*, the sensor screens bleep and wail, in a parody of Bowman's own tortured and concussed mind. As his overloaded senses return to something like normal, he stares aghast out of the pod's window. But what he sees makes him think that he must surely be mad.

He's in a hotel bedroom suite. Or rather, he can *see* himself standing outside the pod. Now, suddenly, he is one and the same as the *alter ego* he has seen. Stunned out of his wits, he explores the gleaming room, all the more alien for its apparent ordinariness. If anything, it is remarkable only for the rather expensive vulgarity of its furnishings. Could it perhaps be an alien idea of what a typical human might want to find at the end of such a journey as this? Some fantasy of luxurious living replicated from an old TV show?

Or perhaps it is an image from Bowman's own mind? Perhaps this is *his* idea of the perfect place to arrive?

But is he a guest, or a prisoner?

The worst is yet to come.

He sees himself in a mirror. He's *old!*

A strange metallic clinking catches his attention. There's somebody in the next room. It's him. Older still. To see this older version of himself is to become that version. The astronaut version of himself disappears, and Bowman, an old gent at dinner, a venerable retired astronaut maybe, is all that remains. Eating a very good meal, from real plates, drinking real wine. But he still manages to break a wine glass on the floor. Mankind is eternally clumsy, it seems.

The slab appears at the foot of a bed, from where Bowman, now aged beyond all recognition, dimly reaches out an arm. The desiccated

# an incredible journey beyond the infinite

space voyager starts to change. His body is transformed into something—not older this time, but younger, much younger. A body at its first defining moment. Not even a child, but a *pre*-child, a developed foetus.

Bowman is a child again. Or perhaps, a child for the first time? A child of the new species?

He launches himself into the darkness of the Monolith, and out into the universe.

The reborn voyager returns from his long and dangerous odyssey, to gaze once again at his first home, the blue planet Earth.

**Heaven and hell:**
*Bowman sets off on the final stage of his odyssey (above). His pod is swallowed up by the Stargate (top right) and he emerges in a strange hotel room (bottom right). This eerie place may have been created from images or memories inside Bowman's own head.*

**On April 13, 1968 the critic Penelope Gilliatt wrote this perceptive review of Kubrick's *2001* for the *New Yorker* magazine.**

I think Stanley Kubrick's "2001: A Space Odyssey" is some sort of a great film, and an unforgettable endeavor. Technically and imaginatively, what he put into it is staggering: five years of his life; his novel and screenplay, with Arthur C. Clarke; his production, his direction, his special effects; his humour and stamina and particular disquiet. The film is not only hideously funny—like "Dr Strangelove"—about human speech and response at a point where they have begun to seem computerized, and where more and more people sound like recordings left on while the soul is out. It is also a uniquely poetic piece of sci-fi, made by a man who truly possesses the drives of both science and fiction.

Kubrick's tale of quest in the year 2001, which eventually takes us to the moon and Jupiter, begins on prehistoric Earth. Tapirs snuffle over the Valhalla landscape, and a leopard with broken-glass eyes guards the carcass of a zebra in the moonlight. Crowds of apes, scratching and ganging up, are disturbingly represented not by real animals but by actors in costume. They are on the brink of evolving into men, and the overlap is horrible. Their stalking movements are already exactly ours: an old tramp's, drunk, at the end of his tether and fighting mad. Brute fear has been refined into the infinitely more painful capacity for dread. The creatures are so nearly human that they have religious impulses. A slab that they suddenly come upon sends them into panicked reverence as they touch it, and the film emits a colossal din of chanting.

The shock of faith boots them forward a few thousand years, and one of the apes, squatting in front of a bed of bones, picks up his first weapon. In slow motion, the hairy arm

swings up into an empty frame and then down again, and the smashed bones bounce into the air. What makes him do it? Curiosity? What makes people destroy anything, or throw away the known, or set off in spaceships? To see what Nothing feels like, driven by some bedrock instinct that it is time for something else?

The last bone thrown in the air is matched, in the next cut, to a spaceship at the same angle. It is now 2001. The race has survived thirty-three years more without extinction, though not with any growth of spirit. There are no negroes in this vision of America's space program; conversation with Russian scientists is brittle with manly terror, and the Chinese can still be dealt with only by pretending they're not there. But technological man has advanced no end. A space way station shaped like a Ferris wheel and housing a hotel called the Orbiter Hilton hangs off the pocked old cheek of Earth. The sound track, bless its sour heart, meanwhile thumps out "The Blue Danube" to confer a little of the courtliness of bygone years on space. The civilization that Kubrick sees coming has the brains of a nuclear physicist and the sensibility of an airline hostess smiling through an oxygen-mask demonstration.

Kubrick is a clever man. The grim joke is that life in 2001 is only faintly more gruesome in its details of sophisticated affluence than it is now. When we first meet William Sylvester as a space scientist, for instance, he is in transit to the moon, via the Orbiter Hilton, to investigate another of the mysterious slabs. The heroic man of intellect is given a nice meal on the way—a row of spacecraft foods to suck through straws out of little plastic cartons, each decorated with a picture of

sweet corn, or whatever, to tell him that sweet corn is what he is sucking. He is really going through very much the same ersatz form of the experience of being well looked-after as the foreigner who arrives at an airport now with a couple of babies, reads in five or six languages that he is welcome, and then finds that he has to manage his luggage and the babies without actual help from a porter.

The scientist of 2001 is only more inured. He takes the inanities of space personnel on the chin. "Did you have a pleasant flight?" Smile, smile. Another smile, possibly pre-filmed, from a girl on a television monitor handling voiceprint identification at Immigration. The Orbiter Hilton is decorated in fresh plumbing-white, with magenta armchairs shaped like pelvic bones scattered through it. Artificial gravity is provided by centrifugal force; inside the rotating Ferris wheel people have weight. The architecture gives the white floor of the Orbiter Hilton's conversation area quite a gradient, but no one lets slip a sign of humor about the slant. The citizens of 2001 have forgotten how to joke and resist, just as they have forgotten how to chat, speculate, grow intimate, or interest one another. But otherwise everything is splendid. They lack the mind for acknowledging that they have managed to diminish outer space into the ultimate in humdrum, or for dealing with the fact that they are spent and insufficient, like the apes.

The film is hypnotically entertaining, and it is funny without once being gaggy, but it is also rather harrowing. It is as eloquent about what is missing from the people of 2001 as about what is there. The characters seem isolated almost beyond endurance. Even in the most absurd scenes, there is often a fugitive melancholy—as astronauts solemnly watch themselves on homey BBC interviews seen millions of miles from Earth, for instance, or as they burn their fingers on their space meals, prepared with the utmost scientific care but a shade too hot to touch, or as they plod around a centrifuge to get some exercise, shadowboxing alone past white coffins where the rest of the crew hibernates in deep freeze.

Separation from other people is total and unmentioned. Kubrick has no characters in the film who are sexually related, nor any close friends. Communication is stuffy and guarded, made at the level of men together on committees or of someone being interviewed. The space scientist telephones his daughter by television for her birthday, but he has nothing to say, and his wife is out; an astronaut on the nine-month mission to Jupiter gets a pre-recorded birthday message from his parents. That's the sum of intimacy. No enjoyment—only the mechanical celebration of the anniversaries of days when the race perpetuated itself.

Again, another astronaut takes a considerable risk to try to save a fellow spaceman, but you feel it hasn't anything to do with affection or with courage. He has simply been trained to save an expensive colleague by a society that has slaughtered instinct. Fortitude is a matter of programming, and companionship seems lost. There remains only longing, and this is buried under banality, for English has finally been booted to death. Even informally, people say "Will that suffice?" for "Will that do?" The computer on the Jupiter spaceship—a chatty, fussy genius called Hal, which has nice manners and a rather querulous need for reassurance about being wanted—talks more like a human being than any human being does in the picture. Hal runs the craft, watches over the rotating quota of men in deep freeze, and plays chess. He gives a lot of thought to how he strikes others, and sometimes carries on about himself like a mother fussing on the telephone to keep a bored grown child hanging on. At a low ebb and growing paranoid, he tells a hysterical lie about a faulty piece of equipment to recover the crew's respect, but a less emotional twin computer on Earth coolly picks him up on the judgement and degradingly defines it as a mistake. Hal, his mimic humanness perfected, detests the witnesses of his humil-

iation and restores his ego by vengeance. He manages to kill all the astronauts but Keir Dullea, including the hibernating crew members, who die in the most chillingly modern death scene imaginable: warning lights simply signal "Computer Malfunction," and sets of electrophysiological needles above the sleepers run amok on the graphs and then record the straight lines of extinction.

The survivor of Hal's marauding self-justification, alone on the craft, has to battle his way into the computer's red-flashing brain, which is the size of your living room, to unscrew the high cerebral functions. Hal's sophisticated voice gradually slows and he loses his grip. All he can remember in the end is how to sing "Daisy"—which he was taught at the start of his training long ago—grinding down like an old phonograph. It is an upsetting image of human decay from command into senility. Kubrick makes it seem a lot worse than a berserk computer being controlled with a screwdriver.

The startling metaphysics of the picture are symbolized in the slabs. It is curious that we should all still be so subconsciously trained in apparently distant imagery. Even to atheists, the slabs wouldn't look simply like girders. They immediately have to do with Mosaic tablets or druidical stones. Four million years ago, says the story, an extra-terrestrial intelligence existed. The slabs are its manifest sentinels. The one we first saw on prehistoric Earth is like the one discovered in 2001 on the moon. The lunar finding sends out an upper-harmonic shriek to Jupiter and puts the scientists on the trail of the forces of creation. The surviving astronaut goes on alone and Jupiter's influence pulls him into a world where time and space are relative in ways beyond Einstein. Physically almost pulped, seeing visions of the planet's surface that are like chloroform nightmares and that sometimes turn into close-ups of his own agonized eyeball and eardrum, he then suddenly lands, and he is in a tranquilly-furnished repro Louis XVI room. The shot of it through the window of his space pod is one of the most heavily charged things in the whole picture, though its effect and its logic are hard to explain.

In the strange, fake room, which is movingly conventional, as if the most that the ill man's imagination can manage in conceiving a better world beyond the infinite is to

recollect something he has once been taught to see as beautiful in a grand decorating magazine, time jumps and things disappear. The barely surviving astronaut sees an old grandee from the back, dining on the one decent meal in the film; and when the man turns around it is the astronaut himself in old age. The noise of the chair moving on the white marble in the silence is typical of the brilliantly selective sound track. The old man drops his wineglass, and then sees himself bald and dying on the bed, twenty or thirty years older still, with his hand up to another of the slabs, which has appeared in the room and stands more clearly than ever for the forces of change. Destruction and creation co-exist in them. They are like Siva.

The last shot of the man is totally transcendental, but in spite of my resistance to mysticism I found it stirring. It shows an X-ray-like image of the dead man's skull recreated as a baby, and approaching Earth. His eyes are enormous. He looks like a mutant. Perhaps he is the first of the needed new species.

It might seem a risky notion to drive sci-fi into magic. But, as with "Strangelove," Kubrick has gone too far and made it the poetically just place to go. He and his collaborator have found a powerful idea to impel space conquerors whom puny times have robbed of much curiosity. The hunt for the remnant of a civilization that has been signalling the existence of its intelligence to the future for four million years, tirelessly stating the fact that it occurred, turns the shots of emptied, comic, ludicrously dehumanized men into something more poignant. There is a hidden parallel to the shot of the ape's arm swinging up into the empty frame with its first weapon, enthralled by the liberation of something to do; I keep remembering the shot of the space scientists asleep in a craft with the "Weightless Condition" sign turned on, his body fixed down by his safety belt while one arm floats free in the air.

# a transformation into...

**A nightmarish journey:**
Bowman flies over a totally alien
landscape (above) and then
passes the rest of his mortal life
in an eerie hotel room, growing
old, collapsing into senility and
then dying—perhaps—only
to be reborn.

# ...the first of the 'needed new species'?

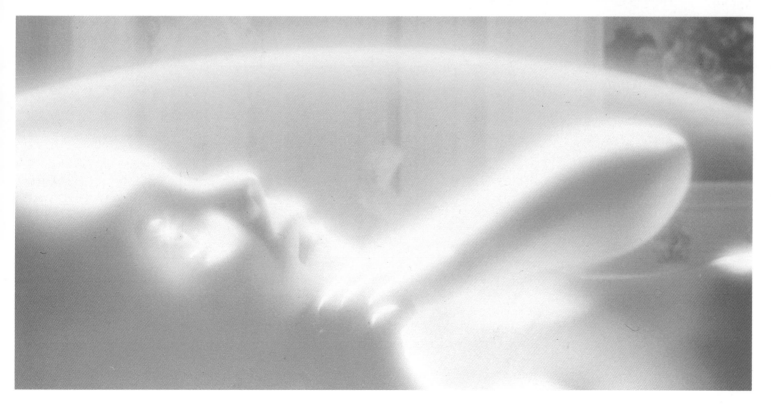

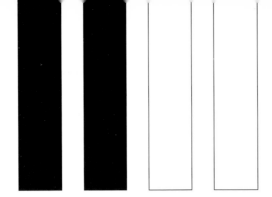

# 3: a meeting of minds

IN MARCH 1964, Stanley Kubrick wrote a letter to Arthur C. Clarke in Ceylon, stating that he wanted to make 'the proverbial good science fiction movie'. He wanted to explore the big questions of the universe: Are we alone? Are there other civilizations in space? Will we ever get the chance to meet them? Up until now, cinema's only response to these deep questions had been to produce movies portraying alien creatures as bug-eyed monsters with their evil green hearts set on the destruction of Earth. The SF movie genre as a whole was fairly disreputable, with one or two notable exceptions. Kubrick, however, was determined to make a serious space film. As far as he was concerned, questions about our place in the cosmos were of very great philosophical importance.

In fact, this intense and highly intelligent film maker had been brooding on such matters for some while. Alexander Walker (film critic for the London *Evening Standard*) remembers meeting him in 1957 in connection with *Paths of Glory*. As Walker prepared to leave the director's Lower East Side apartment, after a long and friendly discussion, a consignment of films arrived for Kubrick's inspection. They turned out to be Japanese SF titles. Kubrick was familiarizing himself with their special effects.

'Are you making a film about outer space?' Walker asked.

Kubrick shot him a dark, suspicious glance:

'*Please!* Be careful what you write.'

Walker kept this intriguing little incident secret for nearly a decade, until it became clear at last that Kubrick was firmly on the way to completing *2001: A Space Odyssey*.

Arthur Clarke, however, got rather less advance notice. When he first heard from Kubrick, he wasn't familiar with that director's earlier work—though he had admired *Lolita* in 1962.

Film publicist Roger Caras (a close friend of Clarke's) was working at that time for Columbia Pictures, the studio which had backed Kubrick's recently completed *Dr Strangelove*. Kubrick and Caras met for lunch in February 1964, and the rather secretive director let slip a hint that his next project would be about space. 'I'm reading everything by everybody,' he said—a claim that would have come as no surprise to anybody who knew him. But Caras told him to stop wasting time, and cut straight through to the best SF writer of the bunch: Arthur C. Clarke.

'I understand he's a recluse, a nut who lives in a tree in India some place,' Kubrick said.

'Like hell!' Caras retorted, whereupon Kubrick asked enthusiastically to be put in touch.

Arthur C. Clarke was born in 1917, and was brought up on a Somerset farm: an unlikely cradle for a space guru. Early on in life, though, he developed an enthusiasm for tinkering with electrical gizmos and crystal radio sets.

'Scientific Sid', his boyhood friends called him. He would regale them with tales of spaceships and journeys to the far planets, his rich imagination fuelled by the early pulp science fiction magazines. When he was thirteen, his father died from the long-lasting effects of gas poisoning in the First World War. Perhaps the exotic fantasies of early SF compensated young Arthur in some way. Even so, he turned his mind soon enough to the practical problems involved in making such fantasies come true. He became skilled in the complexities of celestial mechanics, electronics and radio theory.

During the Second World War he helped to develop radio talk-down equipment for bombers trying to land in poor weather conditions: the ancestor of today's sophisticated automatic landing systems. He worked alongside the brilliant scientist Luis Alvarez for a while, until Alvarez was called away on mysterious business. (That 'mysterious business' turned out to be the 'Manhattan' atomic bomb project.)

After the war, Clarke became Chairman of the British Interplanetary Society, a band of eccentrics who thought that it might be possible, one day, to send people into space. In 1945 he had combined his knowledge of electrical and radio engineering with his keen interest in rocketry, and dreamed up a scheme to try and make space *profitable*, so that flights to the Moon and onwards to Mars might be completed on the back of money-making projects a little closer to home. He sat down and quite literally invented the notion of the geostationary communications satellite. In October 1945, the magazine *Wireless World* published his article on extra-terrestrial relays—though they were somewhat dubious about putting such 'science fiction' into print.

Today, Clarke will insist on sharing the glory with the practically-minded engineers who had to build these systems and get them into orbit. He hates to be called the 'Father of the Communications Satellite'. He prefers simply to be called the Godfather... Satellite TV and telephone links are vastly profitable today, forming the key component of several multi-billion-dollar industries. Clarke has occasionally wondered about how rich he might have become, had he patented his ideas.

He went on to write widely on space, and soon found a ready market for his fictional pieces, stories and novels. His enthusiasm for scuba diving took him on a trip to Ceylon in 1954, and he decided to settle there. Maybe there was a certain tendency towards reclusiveness influencing his move—after all, England is not always the easiest place for unconventional people to live in, and the cold, windy island can be rather obstinate in the face of new ideas or radical explorations. Clarke wanted to be a citizen of the world, and anyway, Ceylon was very beautiful. He was also recovering from the aftershocks of a brief and unsuccessful marriage.

But far from cutting himself off from people, or hiding up a tree, Clarke received a steady stream of visitors and communicated incessantly by telegram, telephone and letter. Published work poured forth at a tremendous rate, and he would occasionally fly abroad for conferences or to collect some of the many prizes and honours awarded to him over the years. In memory of Kubrick's misapprehension, Clarke has labelled himself a 'failed' recluse.

It's a nice irony that Kubrick may well have felt about *his* homeland the way Clarke sometimes felt about his. In 1965 the director quit America and settled just outside London for good.

Born in 1928, the son of a successful New York doctor, Stanley Kubrick was brought up in the Bronx. He claims that he didn't read a book for pleasure until he was nineteen, and he learned little in school. His extraordinary intellect owes hardly anything to the New York educational system. He is a classic autodidact, a self-taught man. His father gave him a Graflex camera for his thirteenth birthday, and by the time he was seventeen he was earning money as a freelance photographer for *Look* magazine. He would supplement his income playing chess for nickels and dimes: 'A dollar goes a long way when all you are buying with it is food.' At twenty-one he had completed his first movie short, a black and white documentary about a middleweight boxer.

Kubrick's first feature film was *Fear and Desire* (1953), a drama of soldiers trapped behind enemy lines. The determined young would-be director borrowed $9,000 from his family and friends. The major film distributors weren't interested in his work, but he got a screening at the Guild Theatre in New York, where critics first had a chance to discover his talent and to encourage further efforts.

Then came *Killer's Kiss* (1955), a dark romance about a boxer who rescues his girlfriend from the attentions of a rapacious nightclub boss. More tangible success arrived in 1956 with *The Killing*, a tight, edgy robbery caper movie (co-produced with an early colleague, James B. Harris). After two low-budget early efforts, Kubrick at last attracted the backing and promotion of a major film studio, United Artists. This time his budget was $200,000. Sterling Hayden played a robber assembling a minutely-detailed racetrack heist, only to have the whole thing come to nothing after a series of apparently insignificant failures and emotional betrayals.

*Paths of Glory*, completed in 1958, starred Kirk Douglas as a French army officer caught up in the futile slaughters of the First World War, with senior officers deliberately sacrificing the lives of their men for petty career victories. Kubrick shot most of it in and around Munich, thus beginning his inexorable drift away from America. Savagely cynical by the standards of the 1950s, it was banned for many years in France, and in all US military bases around the world. The American authorities thought they could detect a 'liberal' slant to the movie. Of course, they entirely missed the point. Or did they? Perhaps the mirror they were looking into was too clear for their liking. At any rate, *Paths of Glory* was completely without political, emotional or moral bias. It was just *there*—a study of war and human moral inadequacy. Only Kubrick's dark humour tempered its remorseless dispassion. (Any fans of *2001*'s equally dispassionate objectivity would do well to seek out *Paths of Glory* for its similar precisions.)

After this, Douglas asked Kubrick to direct him in a big-budget star vehicle, *Spartacus* (1960), which enabled the still remarkably young director to enter the Hollywood mainstream. 'That kid'll go far,' said Douglas. *Spartacus* boosted Kubrick's career and gave him access to the full panoply of Hollywood special effects,

**A deleted lunar world:**
*Scenes of family and social life in the moonbase were edited from the film. Kubrick's two little daughters can be seen at their painting easels.*

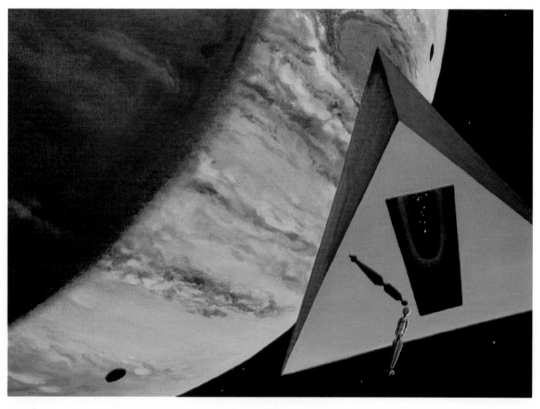

**A tunnel full of stars:**
*Richard McKenna's pre-production artwork shows an alien tetrahedron in orbit above Jupiter, with a tiny spaceship 'Discovery' alongside. There are stars inside the gateway, as in the novel.*

casting and set construction, but he felt that he had been creatively compromised by the whole thing, and he resolved to be his own producer-director in future. He was determined to gain total control over his films, and became remarkable as one of the few directors capable of putting together multi-million-dollar projects without interference from external producers.

Until recently, Kubrick all but disowned *Spartacus,* though in 1991 he prepared a fresh print with additional sequences and a fresh soundtrack. (Even the prodigal child receives its parent's attention.) The nature of his deal with the devil becomes all too clear in the 1960 publicity brochures for *Spartacus*: Kirk Douglas this, Kirk Douglas that—it's all Kubrick can do just to get a *mention*. He was unhappy, as well, about being forced to give precedence to the usual tinsel-town banalities, over and above the genuine historical truths of a bloody slave rebellion (though it was Kubrick who imposed the crucifixion of Spartacus, despite any clear historical evidence that this was how the slave leader was actually killed). For all its compromises, the film is among the most intelligent

and impressive of its genre: the Hollywood historical extravaganza.

1962 saw the completion of *Lolita*, with James Mason and Peter Sellers, based on the controversial novel by Vladimir Nabokov. Its story of an ageing professor's obsession with a teenage nymphet caused consternation and outrage, in more or less that order. The fuss generated in America by the dark sexual overtones of *Lolita* spurred Kubrick into completing most of the project in England, where he found it easier to work than in America. (In the film, he also added two or three years to Lolita's scandalously slender total of elapsed birthdays.)

Like Clarke, Stanley Kubrick became something of a recluse—though perhaps not so much of a 'failed' one: Alexander Walker has described him as 'the most private man I know'.

Major success came with *Dr Strangelove* (1964), a dark comedy of nuclear madness which caught the mood of the times perfectly, quite apart from being a visually and narratively gripping film. Once again Kubrick set up the deal in the USA, and then retreated to England to complete the actual shooting.

**First screening:**
*Arthur Clarke at the Washington premiere, flanked by actors Gary Lockwood (left) and Keir Dullea.*

There is no last-minute cinematic reprieve in *Strangelove*. Mankind blows itself to damnation with the help of maverick machinery, while emotionally retarded political and military leaders consider the merits of going into underground bunkers with a selection of nubile young girls. The film was a frighteningly plausible vision of men and machines in terminal chaos. It was also mercilessly funny. Kubrick was acclaimed as the Best Director of 1964 by the New York critics. Undoubtedly he had become a leading light of American cinema, even if he did insist on filming his work abroad.

By the spring of that same year, Arthur Clarke had learned the hard way to be sanguine about the movie business. He was well aware that most putative film projects tended to fizzle out, never actually making it to the screen. Kubrick's request for a meeting seemed no more significant than any of the other dozens of 'maybes' that kept cropping up from various producers and directors, only to come to nothing in the end.

But Clarke was due to visit New York anyway, in connection with his latest publishing project, *Man and Space*, for Time-Life. ('Excuse me, but what is your authority for this statement?' his editors often asked. 'I am,' Clarke would reply.) A meeting with Kubrick was easy enough to schedule, and was unlikely to disturb his other commitments. Or so he thought.

When Clarke first saw *Strangelove* (in London, while visiting relatives on his way to New York) he was particularly impressed by Kubrick's bravura handling of all the complex machinery. Give or take the odd few million deaths (as General Turgidson might say) it's a relatively small step from an equipment-laden nuclear bomber to its close cousin, the nuclear-powered spaceship. Kubrick's film augured well for an even more ambitious project, Clarke decided. Notwithstanding his brilliantly far-sighted imagination, Scientific Sid couldn't possibly have guessed what he was letting himself in for: a three-year stretch working alongside the film world's most extraordinary, most demanding genius.

The two men met for the first time at Trader Vic's restaurant in New York's Plaza Hotel on April 22, 1964. Kubrick's sharp intelligence was the second thing which Clarke noticed about him. He could soak up new ideas almost instantly, and seemed to forget nothing, no matter how apparently trivial. He asked incessant questions, and stored the resultant answers away like a computer. But the *first* thing about him that Clarke noticed was his 'night person's pallor'. Kubrick was a man who functioned best in the very small hours of the morning. He came across as a quiet, rather shy man, but with a laser-like intellect and a huge curiosity about the world and everything in it—or beyond it.

This first meeting between what *Life* magazine once described as 'two marathon cerebrators' went very well. They spent eight solid hours together, talking over ideas, with the conversation ranging from space exploration to politics, from flying saucers to Senator Goldwater. There were certainly some possibilities to explore, though Clarke fervently hoped that whatever all this might lead to, it wouldn't keep him away from his beautiful retreat for too long. He was very settled where he was, exploring the underwater reefs near his home, and generally enjoying the quiet life of a tropical islander. New York was certainly an exciting change, but he had found that the glamour of this great city tended to wear off after about fifteen minutes...

Over the next month Clarke and Kubrick met regularly, for five hours or so at a time, virtually every day. They chatted over lunches, dinners and breakfasts. They earnestly dissected the latest theories in science, space and high technology during visits to movie theatres, art galleries, restaurants and bars, or at Kubrick's apartment. And they watched screenings of the competition—George Pal's highly impressive *Destination Moon*, scripted by another SF heavyweight, Robert Heinlein, with technical assistance from the rocket scientist Hermann Oberth; *War of the Worlds*, with its competent special effects; *Forbidden Planet*, the very first big-budget colour space fiction film; and *The Day the Earth Stood Still*, a dramatic, moralistic tale of alien intervention in our terrestrial warmongering. But Kubrick expressed severe criticisms about all the space films they screened.

He deprecated their lack of absolute realism, their failure to examine what space travel might *really* be like; and although *Destination Moon*'s almost documentary approach to its subject was striking for its time, Kubrick felt that none of these films had touched on the real philosophical importance of space travel, or its impact on society as a whole.

He screened Alexander Korda's 1936 epic, *Things to Come*, which he sat through, but hated: 'What are you trying to do to me? I'll never see another movie you recommend,' he complained to Clarke. (By an odd quirk of fate, *2001* was destined to be photographed on some of the very same studio lots once commandeered by Korda.) Kubrick reckoned that his new colleague was too much in thrall to science fiction romance, too uncritical of the genre. Interesting then, to note that Clarke found Kubrick 'in some danger of believing in UFOs', and took great care to disabuse the director of some of *his* unrealistic notions.

Thus, two great egos confronted each other head-to-head, sometimes in agreement, sometimes in remorseless combat. A brilliant, if occasionally unstable partnership was about to be forged. There would be times ahead when Clarke would find himself wishing he had ended up working *anywhere* but in the same world as Stanley Kubrick; yet there's no doubt that these two men formed some kind of an attachment right from the start. Today they still flirt occasionally with the idea of working together again. 'God forbid!' jokes Clarke; 'If that happened, I would have to go in the Guinness Book of Records as the only writer in the world ever to work with Stanley Kubrick twice!' They also go through regular phases during which, according to various reports, 'Arthur isn't talking to Stanley at the moment.' These glitches tend not to last very long. Clarke still corresponds with the director regularly, often to the point of investigating new screenplays. And for his part, Kubrick has stated frequently that 'One of the most fruitful and enjoyable collaborations I have had was with Arthur C. Clarke.'

They are deeply fond of each other, even though most of their half-hearted attempts at professional reunion tend to evaporate whenever Clarke considers the merest possibility of ending up under Kubrick's command again. If only he could do all the work from Sri Lanka, and be *quite* sure that Stanley wouldn't bother him on the telephone after nine o'clock at night...

Roger Caras, who first introduced the two men, knew Kubrick well from the *Dr Strangelove* days, and he is also a good friend of Clarke's: 'Arthur has a tremendous ego, and quite rightly, because of his many accomplishments. In fact that was one of his nicknames some while back, I believe: 'Ego'. But he loves taking pride in what he's done, and I think that's a wonderful thing. Now, I've never seen Arthur take a back seat to anybody in his entire life, except for Stanley... But I believe Stanley was also very impressed by Arthur. When those two were together, bouncing ideas off each other, it was like watching two intellectual duellists.'

During those early, heady meetings, neither of them had any idea that their pet project would take so long to complete, nor that it would be so difficult and so complex to achieve. 'Our initial schedule was hilariously optimistic,' recalls Clarke. Kubrick reckoned they could wrap the whole thing up in about two years, and asked Clarke formally to assist in writing the script. They shook hands on the deal during the evening of May 17, 1964, then wandered out onto the veranda of Kubrick's apartment to look at the cityscape, aglow with its evening lights, and immediately saw the most spectacular UFO flitting across the sky over Manhattan. It turned out to be reflected light from ECHO 1, a large silver balloon launched into space as part of an American radio experiment. Clarke's famous theories of satellite communication were being tested for real.

It occurred to Kubrick that it might be a good idea to insure his project against the commercially damaging possibility of an *actual* alien encounter. If any flying saucers touched down while his film was in production, the whole thing would be rendered laughably obsolete in an instant. Kubrick's motto: 'Don't save the day. Anticipate it.' Lloyds of London suggested a rather high premium, which the director eventually rejected. (How, wondered Clarke, had the insurance company made their calculations?

What kind of actuarial tables could they possibly have used?)

Clarke resigned himself to a sojourn away from Ceylon, and got down to work. Kubrick installed him in front of a typewriter at his Polaris Productions offices on Central Park West. He survived for nearly an entire day before dashing off to the relative safety of the Chelsea Hotel, downtown on West 23rd Street, where he barricaded himself in for the duration. This particular hostelry is famous for its indulgent cosseting of creative genius. Its brochure of the time advertised 'an oasis of friendliness for people of temperament' and highlighted rooms that were 'large and soundproofed'. Clarke would sometimes wander into the bar for a chat with William Burroughs or Allen Ginsberg, no doubt gaining inspiration from their thoroughly off-beat imaginations. The Chelsea Hotel still likes to boast that the novels *Naked Lunch* and *2001: A Space Odyssey* were written within its walls.

For the script did, indeed, start out as a novel. Kubrick disliked film scripts, except as the most purely technical accompaniment to the film-making process; so he suggested that they should work on a novel first of all, and then extract a cinematic equivalent from that. Scripts, with their dry language of close-ups, long-shots and cuts, were desperately unexciting to write. If they started out with a piece of straight creative prose, they could let their imaginations properly off the leash. And there would be something acceptably readable and exciting to show Kubrick's backers at MGM. Kubrick once said that a typical screenplay is 'the most uncommunicative form of writing ever devised'. But they had to show the studio *something* if they were to receive the obviously enormous backing that would be required.

It's worth noting that such a writing arrangement was distinctly unusual. Ordinarily, a studio or a producer will acquire the rights to a novel and then commission a screenplay broadly based upon it; or else a script will be developed specifically with the cinematic elements in mind, and someone will come along afterwards and convert its major themes into a novel, for marketing purposes—the so-called process of 'novelization'. What Kubrick and Clarke set out to do, however, was to create a novel first, with a film in mind, and then much later to do the drudge work of converting it into a script. They agreed that the film credits for screenwriting should highlight Kubrick, then Clarke, while the subsequent book would highlight Clarke over Kubrick. It was a fair reflection of the truth, with both men writing and contributing ideas, so that it often became impossible to determine who had first thought of what.

Across the history of 2001's production, both novel and script developed simultaneously, the one often feeding from the other. It was a difficult process, and it all took more than twice as long as either Clarke or Kubrick had ever envisaged.

The starting point for the novel was a story called *The Sentinel* which Clarke had written in 1948. It was a clever, concise tale of men discovering an alien machine on the Moon and accidentally triggering its signalling device after its obviously uninterrupted sleep of thousands of years. This, quite recognizably, is the source for 2001's pitch-black Monolith and its eerie radio screech. Clarke had actually written the story for a BBC Christmas competition (it didn't win). The Monolith, Sentinel, or whatever, was a sort of 'cosmic fire alarm' designed to alert an unseen intelligence that human beings had left the cradle of earth and were starting to poke their inquisitive noses into space. But many other ideas are explored in 2001, derived from a wide range of Clarke's work. He has insisted recently that *The Sentinel* 'bears about as much relation to the movie as an acorn to the resultant full-grown oak'.

There were plenty of themes beyond the scope of *The Sentinel* which Kubrick wanted to examine: in particular, day-to-day life aboard an interplanetary spaceship, and the relationship between human beings and their advanced technology. Another concept which soon gained in prominence was that of cosmic interference in our evolutionary history. Perhaps this is not so surprising, given that Clarke had already achieved world-wide acclaim for his novel *Childhood's End* (1953), which brilliantly explores such possibilities. For instance, its major theme is that much of our ancient cultural imagery comes not from mysterious influences

***The banality of realism:***
*A stewardess relaxes in Kubrick's garish space station - a place no less horrible than most of today's airport lounges.*

in our distant past, but rather, from a collective premonition of something that *hasn't happened yet*—the landing on Earth of benign aliens with unfortunately dragon-like exteriors, whose purpose is to prepare us for a glorious end, in which we are supposed to depart from our physical selves and set up home as part of a greater Cosmic Consciousness. The devilish aliens, by the way, turn out to be much more pleasant than their outer shapes might suggest. Indeed, they are positively heroic. By a terrible quirk of fate, they prove incapable of joining us in our psychic adventure and are doomed to become extinct. Meanwhile, the last humans on Earth reach out towards a kind of ultimate cosmic fruition.

This was Clarke in typically optimistic mode. It took Kubrick, fresh from detailing the appalling ludicrousness of nuclear global destruction, to introduce a cooler, more detached vision. What if aliens had indeed tinkered with our prehistoric past, by teaching us how to fashion and use basic tools? In particular, clubs, knives and axes? Here are the ancient precursors of our beloved atomic missiles. Modern human instincts remain essentially thuggish: it's just that their tools and cudgels have developed some-what in complexity. But of course, the irony of it all (so typically Kubrickian) is that these very same aggressive instincts have allowed us to dominate the planet and to reach out into deepest space.

Clarke duly worked in an extensive prehistoric opening to the novel, outlining our primitive ancestors' education under the guidance of some rather more advanced celestial visitors. At first this was a very literal affair: Clarke sug-gested transparent crystals showing 'pictures' demonstrating how an apeman could profitably improve his circumstances, and Kubrick once suggested something along the lines of teaching the apes some kind of 'commando tactics'. Some of these ideas survive in the completed and published version of the novel.

The film, however, adopted a broader, more subtle imagery—so subtle, in fact, that quite a lot of people didn't fully understand the con-nection between the mysterious black slab and the apeman Moonwatcher's sudden interest in old bones.

For a long time there was considerable un-certainty as to whether or not an encounter with the mysterious alien pillar should be the grand finale, or the start of the movie. Nor was it easy to work out an ending, or to think up any kind of confrontation between astronauts and aliens.

One thing Clarke and Kubrick agreed on straight away: if aliens were indeed to look genuinely *alien*, they had to be effectively incom-prehensible to the audience. By definition, anything we can more or less recognize is ob-viously not so very alien to us after all. That traditional SF movie monster, the man in a rubber suit, was right out of the frame. This was a tricky problem, conveniently side-stepped many months later when the potent imagery of the black slabs provided an opportunity to dispense with physical aliens altogether. Obviously, such all-powerful creatures had advanced far beyond their ancient corporeal identities.

Clarke was ready with a first, albeit rough, version of the novel by Christmas of that first year, 1964. This enabled Kubrick to set up a film deal with MGM, who made a formal announce-ment on February 22, 1965 that they were to finance Stanley Kubrick's *Journey Beyond the Stars*, to be filmed on location around the world (so they thought then) and at the giant MGM studios at Borehamwood, north London. Clarke thought he could see the beginning of the end. He had no idea he would still be polishing the manuscript two years later.

The title, *2001: A Space Odyssey*, appears to have been entirely Kubrick's idea, and was certainly an improvement on the *Journey* 'working title'. The Odyssean element, however, appears to have been in their minds from an early stage, though Clarke has acknowledged that it took both of them an extraordinarily long time to see the obvious—that only *one* of their five astral explorers should survive for the final encounter. Clarke's book *The Lost Worlds of 2001* reproduces a selection of rejected themes and deleted chapters from the novel, including any number of combinations of crew members getting killed, or most of the crew surviving. Some of the early 'accidents' seem distinctly tortuous, relying rather heavily on a series of improbably disastrous equipment failures.

In *The Lost Worlds* Clarke recounts that his sessions with Kubrick, though mainly deadly serious, would occasionally collapse into farce as they struggled to find an end for their movie:

*MAY 31 (1964) One hilarious idea we won't use. Seventeen aliens—featureless black pyramids—riding in open cars down Fifth Avenue, surrounded by Irish cops.*

A year later, they were still struggling. But by mid-1965 Clarke had pronounced himself 'cautiously encouraged' about his latest idea: that astronaut Dave Bowman should regress to infancy at the end of the film. Radical notions of allowing the entire crew to survive and turn into starchildren, crawling about in some gigantic cosmic playpen, were quickly eliminated.

There remained the problem of killing off most of the crew, so that a lonesome Dave Bowman could be allowed to reach his Odyssean apotheosis. (By now, the significant influence of Joseph Campbell's analysis of myth, *The Hero with a Thousand Faces,* was making itself felt. An enthusiastic Kubrick gave a copy to Clarke, and some of the book's ideas seemed very useful.) Of course the tragic, guilt-ridden, prideful and murderous computer HAL 9000 eventually comes along and neatly squares a very inconvenient circle. Here was the modern Minotaur waiting at the heart of his electronic labyrinth.

Hal started life as Athena, a semi-intelligent female computer. One way and another, his role just grew and grew, to the point where he was pretty much the star of the show. Once production had got under way, the Canadian actor Douglas Rain was hired for a fortnight to record Hal's lines, and completed his entire workload over a single long weekend. He never got to see where his lines fitted into the big scheme of things until he saw the movie on its release. (Kubrick was so secretive, very few of his actors and crew knew where the script was heading from one day to the next, and Rain was no exception.) As it turned out, his voice was perfect for the part. Earlier on, Kubrick had recorded some sequences with the voice of Martin Balsam (one of the jurors in *Twelve Angry Men*) but Balsam's voice came over as slightly too emotional.

Kubrick was fascinated by the implications of computers and Artificial Intelligence, and Clarke has long propounded his theory that humans and computers will one day become all but indistinguishable, as our ever-advancing technology supersedes natural evolution and comes up with some kind of symbiotic breed. In the far future, 'we will not travel in spaceships. We will *be* spaceships.'

Hal—a computer, remember—got the best and funniest line of the entire movie: 'I know I've made some poor decisions recently, but I'm feeling much better now.' Pretty rich stuff, coming from a megalomaniac paranoid depressive who's just committed multiple murder. Hal's emergence as a major player was surely Kubrick's doing. As a general rule, anything in

*2001* which smacks of laughter in the dark is Kubrick having his fun with us. Clarke's work is capable of considerable poignancy, but he has at least *some* degree of faith in humanity's potential to win out in the end. Most of his novels, after all, are nothing short of manifestos for social and scientific progress. With Kubrick, the odds on mankind making it to the winning post are a little longer. He places a sneaky bet on the Doomsday machines.

The odds were pretty long, as well, on Arthur working with *l'enfant terrible* Stanley for months at a time without occasionally wanting to scream. Certain tensions developed between these two brilliant men, it has to be said. Hardly surprising, given the enormous pressure that Kubrick was under, trying to keep a huge production under control. In July 1966, deep in dreary north London, far away from his island paradise, and with Kubrick still demanding revisions, Clarke was beginning to wonder if it was all worth it. Most frustrating of all, Kubrick continued to hinder publication of the novel, which, he said, still needed more work.

A publishing deal had been set up, in principle at least, with Delacorte Press in the USA. They had placed costly advertisements in the book trade journals, and had gone to the additional expense of setting the novel in type, ready for the printing of galley proofs. Clarke's literary agent Scott Meredith had negotiated a very handsome $160,000 package, predicated on Delacorte being able to get a hardback out before the film's release, and then doing a paperback tie-in once the movie got into its stride. Kubrick, however, wouldn't sign on the dotted line. It would be another two years before Clarke finally saw his novel in print, as the *2001* production dragged on, over time and over budget.

At last, the novel was published by New American Library in the summer of 1968, not quite in time for the film's initial release. Kubrick finally signed a contract with just four weeks to go before the movie opened in Washington and New York, and not a single copy of the book yet printed. (Delacorte Press was obliged to throw away all the expensive proofs and printing plates they'd already prepared in 1966, because their contract was never signed.) Despite the publishing world's reluctance to sanction a movie tie-in so long *after* a premiere, bidding was still brisk, with NEL pitching in at around $130,000 (though Delacorte's enthusiasm had waned somewhat, and they dropped out of the bidding, still licking their wounds from the expensive fiasco of July 1966).

'Don't worry,' Kubrick reassured a frustrated Clarke; 'Everything will work out in the end.'

And it did. Arguably, the novel turned out better for Kubrick's incessant demands for improvements; and it sold in enormous numbers, despite its delayed arrival. *2001* was still on its first run in some theatres as much as two years later, and the fuss didn't really die down for a long time. There was ample opportunity to market the book. (Sales to date, under various imprints: four million copies, and still climbing.)

In retrospect, it is tempting to imagine that Kubrick's reluctance to allow publication earlier on was due, in part at least, to his desire to deny audiences any warning of what they were about to see. He wanted them to work out the implications of his film for themselves, without benefit of Clarke's crisp, poetic exposition. Kubrick had maintained a very high level of security throughout the shooting, and at all his interviews he had stressed his desire that people should view *2001* as a 'non-verbal experience'. One can hardly be surprised at his desire to see if his Great Experiment had really worked on its own terms. But he has always claimed, most insistently, that it was sheer pressure of work which prevented him from paying attention to the book's final proofs and contract until the movie itself was firmly in the can and ready for release.

Arthur Clarke doesn't like to dwell on the painful financial inconvenience which Kubrick's intransigence caused him prior to everything 'working out' after April 1968: 'Well, you know, Stanley is Stanley.' Fortunately for both men, profits from the book remain good. More recently, *2010* and *2061: Odyssey III* sold in huge numbers. Kubrick has a share in all the sequel novels, and in any marketing or film right deals related to *2001*. As a very happy Arthur said back in 1968, 'Stanley and I are laughing all the way to the bank!'

**To Jupiter and beyond:**
*Robert McCall's publicity artwork shows Dave Bowman jetting off towards the unknown, at the climax of Kubrick and Clarke's epic 'little movie.'*

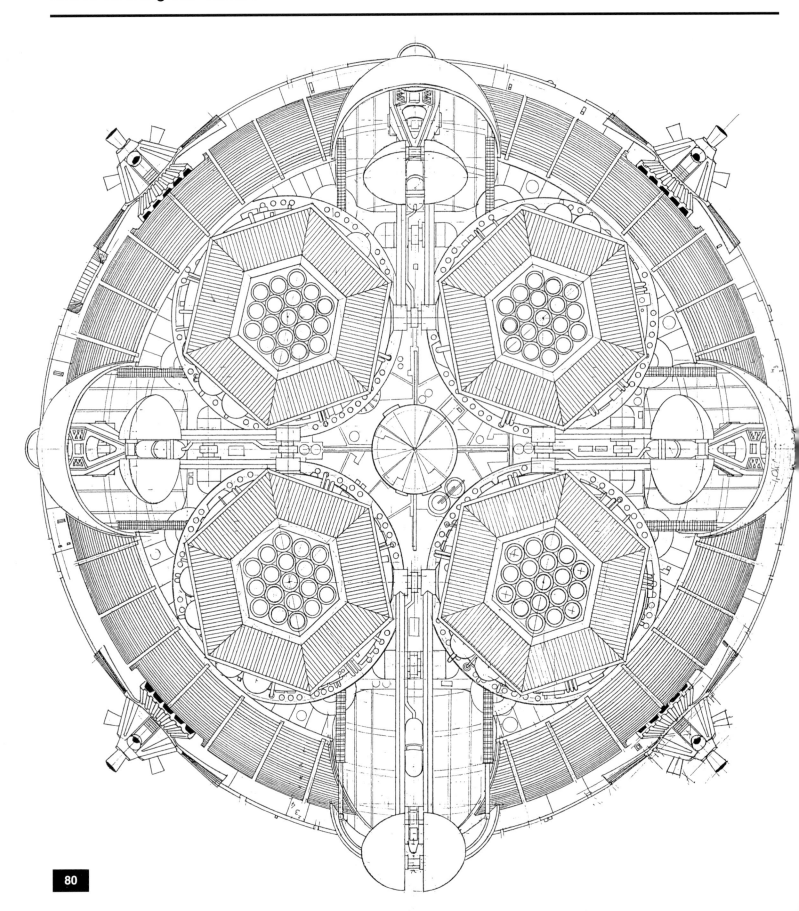

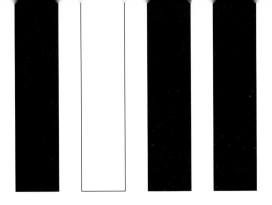

# 4: shipbuilding

**The business end:**
*This detailed drawing of the 'Aries' lunar lander underside shows the engines and landing gear, and is typical of the countless thousands of construction plans which were drawn up during production.*

NOW THAT THE story was beginning to take shape, Kubrick had to start thinking about the visual elements of his project. Nobody really knew for sure what the space vehicles of the year 2001 would look like, or how they would operate. Kubrick wanted absolute realism: he wanted the hardware on screen to look as though it really *worked*. But who would create all this machinery? Traditional film artists and set designers could hardly be expected to know about the arcane details of spaceflight systems. The perfectionist director didn't want his expensive, ambitious movie to be out-guessed by the real future.

Towards the end of January 1965, a good many prominent space writers, scientists and researchers happened to be passing through the New York area all at once, on various errands to do with books, conferences and publicity events. Arthur C. Clarke was in town of course, 'brainstorming' with Kubrick and publicizing *Man and Space* for *Time-Life*; the American Institute of Aeronautics and Astronautics was holding a convention at the New York Hilton; and two men from a small but busy space consultancy company were meeting with publishers in connection with their own book on the theme of extra-terrestrial intelligence: Harry Lange and Frederick Ordway.

Harry H-K Lange had already worked for NASA on advanced space vehicle concepts.

Lange was (indeed still is) a superb draughtsman and colourist. He was also fully conversant with the most highly classified details of propulsion systems, radar navigation, docking techniques, and many other matters preoccupying the US aerospace technologists of the day. His job had been to visualize as-yet-unborn vehicle concepts, so that NASA and its associated army of corporate collaborators could communicate their ideas for the future.

Lange had escaped the ravages of a defeated Germany (when he was fourteen he survived three days in Hamburg during the intense Allied bombing which razed that once beautiful city to the ground). He had wanted to find a country where he could pursue his interests in art and archaeology unhindered by Nazi or Communist oppression. Like many citizens of Europe in those days, harried from pillar to post by zealous armies and unfriendly occupiers, Lange found the freedom he was looking for in America; a rich and accommodating nation eagerly seeking out fresh talent in its burgeoning techno-war against the Russians.

Lange designed pilots' training manuals for the army ('How to Fly Your Helicopter') and then created rocket illustrations for ABMA, the Army Ballistic Missile Agency at Huntsville, Alabama, before joining NASA's Future Projects Division when the civilian agency swallowed up most of the military programmes. But no sooner had he

Spaceplanes such as this Pan-American *Orion* were always part of the 1960's plan. The 'Moon Race' with Russia forced NASA to set aside early development of spaceplanes in favour of disposable (and relatively simpler) rockets.

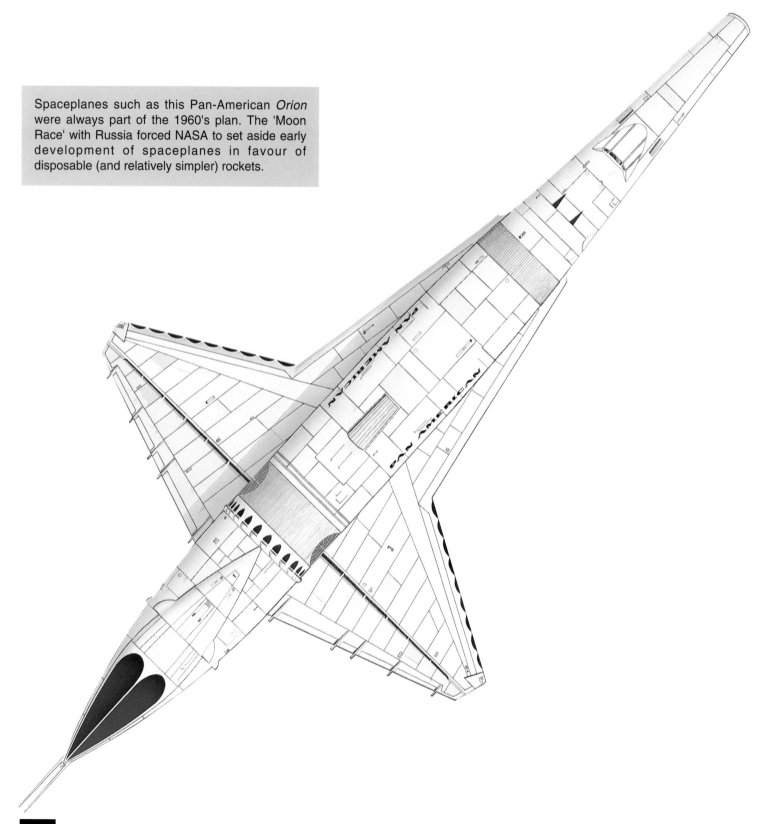

# the rise and fall of a global airline: "we are expecting to fly...

# ...our planes in space by the year 2001"

got into his stride than his promising career was threatened, as the Vietnam conflict started to make inroads on space budgeting. The *Apollo* lunar programme continued unabated; speculative 'future projects' divisions, however, were scaled down. By 1964 both Lange and his close friend Frederick Ordway were wondering about their own futures. They felt it was no longer such a good idea to be tied down so exclusively to the governmental space efforts. They initiated some outside projects of their own.

Frederick Ordway had what might best be described as the gift of the gab. He had already built an outstanding intellectual and commercial career with NASA, with Lange at the ABMA, and with a wide variety of first-rate industrial, uni-

versity and research institutions. His scientific expertise was backed up by a persuasive understanding of the public relations processes by which large and complex organizations like NASA try to inform the outside world about their complex activities. Along with Lange (and three other colleagues) he had also founded a specialist company, the General Astronautics Research Corporation, or GARC, which provided consultancy services in the early, heady days of rocket and missile development, when it seemed that just about every major contractor in the country would be involved somewhere in that field.

Ordway found out that Clarke was in New York, and arranged a social gathering at the Harvard Club, where he and Lange were staying. So: what was Arthur doing in town? Oh,

**The big wheel:**
*The space station concept emerges (right) as a central docking area surrounded by a rim of accommodation blocks, all gently spinning to produce an artificial gravity.*

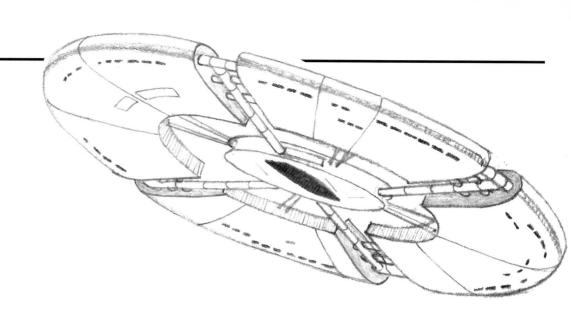

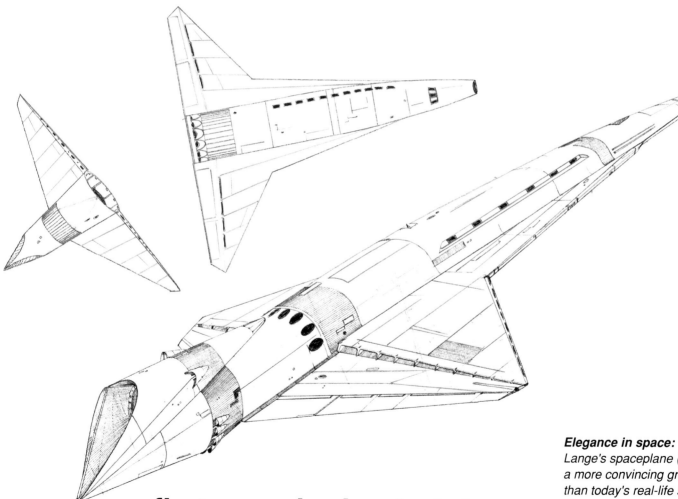

# fly to a spinning hotel 200 miles up in the sky

**Elegance in space:**
*Lange's spaceplane (left) shows a more convincing gracefulness than today's real-life shuttle. The smaller sketch shows how the main body of the plane was supposed to break away from its winged booster.*

publicizing *Man and Space*, and working with a rather talented young movie director called Stanley Kubrick on a film about contact with extra-terrestrials... Clarke explained that this was going to be *the* space movie, against which all others of its kind would be judged. It would portray humanity facing the enormity of the cosmos, and would consider the possibility of other forms of life out there among the stars.

Oh, really? What a coincidence! Lange and Ordway were putting together a book on that very same theme: *Intelligence in the Universe*, for publishers Prentice-Hall, and they'd just completed another book for Dutton: *Life in Other Solar Systems*. Clarke asked to see some of the artwork which Lange had prepared for the new book. He and Ordway then spent a pleasant half-hour or so showing material to Arthur, who certainly seemed impressed. But a dinner date loomed. Ordway and Lange had to make their excuses and get ready for going out.

A little while later they were standing outside the club, waiting for the doorman to hail a cab. It was snowing heavily (this is always the sort of meteorological detail which people remember after so long). Just as they were about to be driven away, one of the club's employees ran out and told Ordway there was an urgent phone call for him. When he reached the telephone, a voice identified itself on the other end of the line:

'Mr Ordway? My name is Stanley Kubrick...'

Clarke, it seems, had left the Harvard Club and trudged through the blizzard to a discreet callbox on Sixth Avenue as soon as his friendly chat with Lange and Ordway was over. He had spoken to Kubrick and urged him to call them personally, before they even had time to leave the club for the evening.

Next day, Lange and Ordway spent what the latter has described as 'a mentally exhilarating afternoon' discussing concepts with Kubrick and Clarke at the director's Lower East Side apartment, and examining the possibility of collaboration. Then they were asked formally for their assistance. Ordway would become principal technical adviser to the movie project and Lange would map out a range of detailed and realistic spaceship configurations. The two of them signed an initial six-month contract to work in New York, from Kubrick's Polaris Productions offices on Central Park West, where they would help to assemble all the necessary technical material, and keep Kubrick informed about the latest trends in real space research.

**Company car:**
*Fred Ordway persuaded major manufacturers to supply props, such as this 1966 concept car from General Motors. It was used as the background for the trite television love scene which sends Heywood Floyd to sleep during his space shuttle trip.*

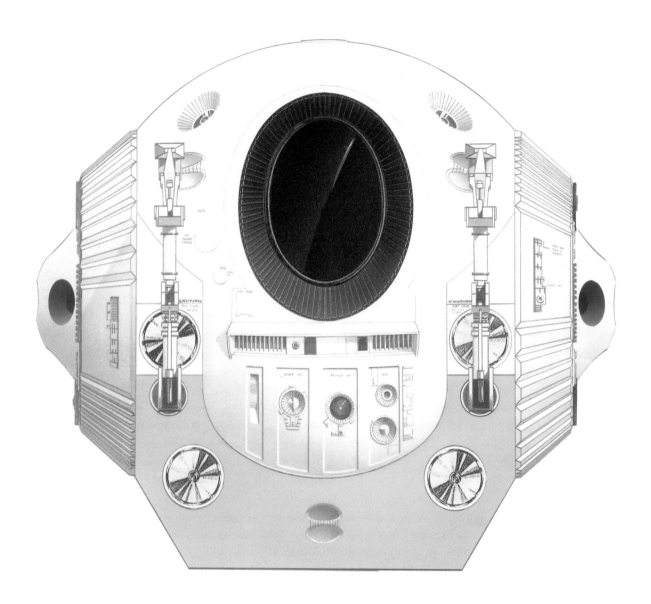

This design for a space repair pod looks very convincing nearly thirty years after the first rough sketches emerged from Lange's drawing board. If it doesn't yet exist, then it certainly should. Illustrator Simon Atkinson spent many weeks recreating the design from film stills.

Notice HAL's malevolent glowing red eye, just off-centre below the main oval window. Other TV cameras are studded around the sphere in conical recesses, so that the nine-foot-diameter pod can be remotely controlled.

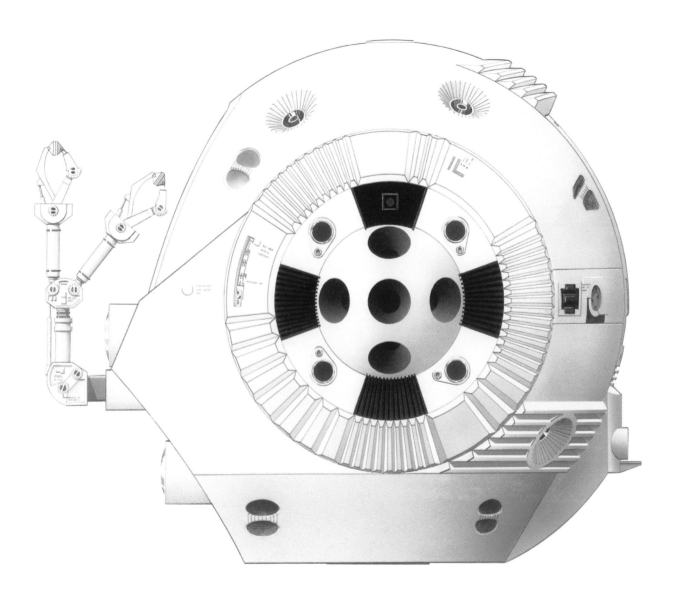

This side view of the pod shows the reaction control motors, the little gas jets which can twist and tumble the pod in any direction. Today, NASA is developing a robot version for use during space station construction.

Lange's experience at the Future Projects Office in Huntsville taught him that hardware had to look consistent with reality. For instance: the ridges and grooves are radiators, and there are plenty of hand-holds for the astronauts. Dozens of draughtsmen and artists worked on the pod's final detailing.

# a lunar lander takes shape

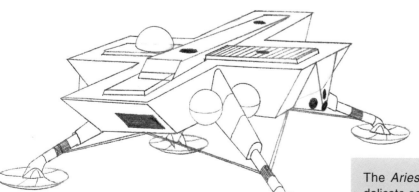

The *Aries* lunar landing vehicle takes shape (this page) in a delicate series of prototype sketches—just a few of many dozens. The final result was the 3-ft model (photograph on the right) which included shock absorbers for the legs and compressed-air jets hidden in the rocket nozzles. Notice the thick steel mounting tube to the right of the picture.

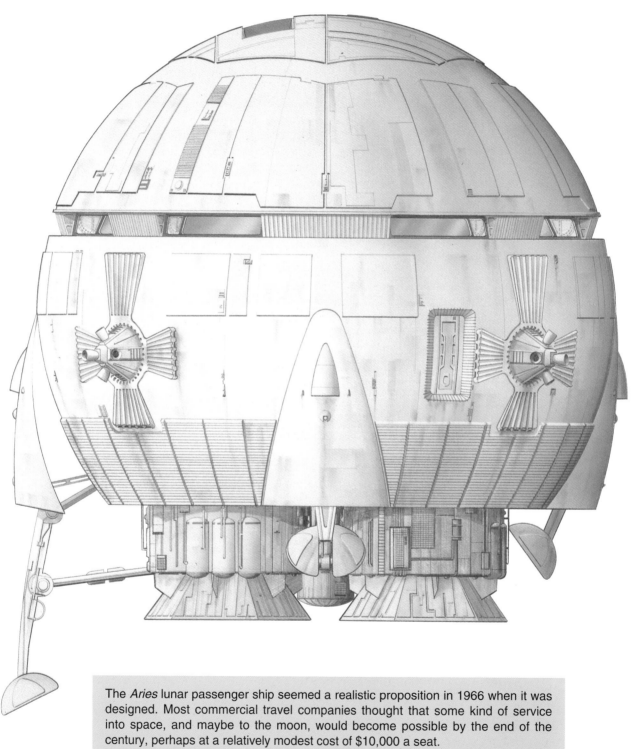

The *Aries* lunar passenger ship seemed a realistic proposition in 1966 when it was designed. Most commercial travel companies thought that some kind of service into space, and maybe to the moon, would become possible by the end of the century, perhaps at a relatively modest cost of $10,000 a seat.

In a very short time—two years—such ideas evaporated, as Vietnam took hold of the American tax budget and Congress began to slash NASA's funds. But all the ships in Kubrick's *2001* look as though they *should* have been built by now.

Lange chafed at being stuck in New York for so long. Of course, neither he nor Fred Ordway had any idea they would be working alongside Kubrick not just for six months, but for the best part of three years. Nor could they guess they'd end up moving both their families across the Atlantic to England as *2001: A Space Odyssey* came to absorb more and more of their working lives. Both men would emerge from their upcoming adventure very different from when they first began it. Their association with the film would stay with them for the rest of their careers. 'He's the guy that worked on *2001*,' people would say of each of them from now on.

Ordway began to open up channels of communication with dozens of real aerospace manufacturing companies. He persuaded them just how good it would be for their own publicity if they were seen to take an interest in Mr Kubrick's new movie. For instance: the Pan American symbol writ large on the side of the *Orion* space liner was not simply the result of some random creative whim. The airline 'starred' on screen in return for informing Kubrick and his advisers about their cherished ambitions for the future (presumably, bankruptcy ten years ahead of the new millennium didn't feature in their plans).

NASA, IBM, Honeywell, Boeing, Bell Telephone, RCA, General Dynamics, Chrysler, General Electric, Grumman: all these corporate giants provided tons of documentation and even real hardware. They presented theoretical outlines, drew up instrument panels, and discussed in the minutest detail how astronauts of the future would spend their days: what kind of buttons they would press; how they would wash, eat and sleep; what kind of pyjamas they might wear.

Not surprisingly, a good number of brand-name logos appear scattered around the *2001* sets. (Nowadays the film industry regards 'product placement' as a valuable source of revenue.) For the contractors, as indeed for an already politically-defensive NASA, Kubrick's *2001* looked well on the way to becoming a wonderful advertisement for space technology.

Most of the companies were happy enough with the way things turned out. Except for IBM.

They spent many months contributing data to the film, and were less than pleased when HAL 9000 turned out to be such a wrong 'un. The whole mess was exacerbated when the press later noticed that the letters HAL were just one notch along the alphabet from IBM. Undoubtedly this was a genuine coincidence. Even so, the world's biggest computer company didn't welcome their association with *2001*'s maverick mainframe, which was portrayed hijacking its own ship and then ruthlessly 'disconnecting' its human end-users. (IBM logos were removed from much of the *Discovery* hardware, though they can still clearly be seen in the *Orion* spaceplane cockpit.)

Kubrick fired questions in every direction, and expected precise answers. What fuel would an interplanetary spaceship use? How big would its radio dish be? How much storage space would be taken up by food and oxygen? What would be the exact sequence of a passenger journey to the moon? How would you rescue people in emergencies? These were tough questions, bearing in mind that NASA and the aerospace companies were only just beginning to work this sort of thing out for themselves. Much of what they told the *2001* team lay on the shadowed boundary between hard knowledge and pure speculation. Meanwhile, a hundred or so miles up in the sky, the early space vehicles were testing out all these fancy theories for real—and for the very first time. Cape Kennedy was struggling to put capsules weighing just a few tons into low Earth orbit for maybe a week or two at a stretch, and Kubrick was demanding to know how a 700-foot nuclear powered spaceship weighing hundreds of tons might safely be despatched to the far planets, with her crew kept alive and healthy for perhaps years at a time.

And at last, after all this data had been gathered, it had to be made to come alive on screen. Production designer Tony Masters came to New York in April 1965. He was a tall, bumbling British public school chap with a bit of a stutter, and an extraordinary talent for sketching ideas and storyboards with lightning speed. By all accounts a marvellous man. Coming out of the army at the end of the Second World War, an ex-major in the Royal Artillery, he was ideally suited to the marshalling

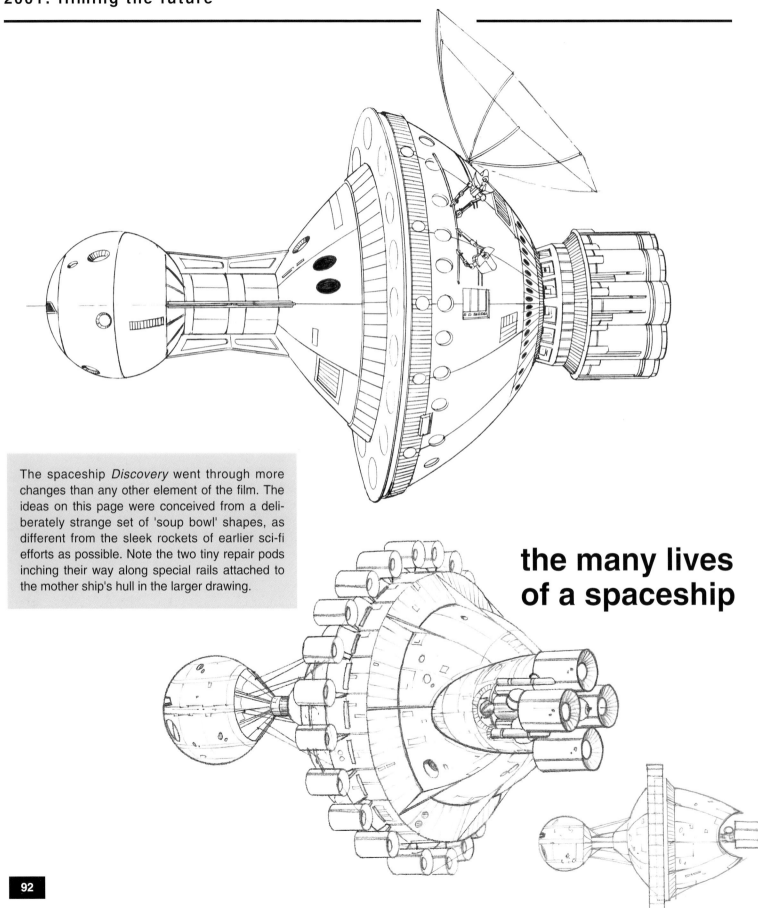

The spaceship *Discovery* went through more changes than any other element of the film. The ideas on this page were conceived from a deliberately strange set of 'soup bowl' shapes, as different from the sleek rockets of earlier sci-fi efforts as possible. Note the two tiny repair pods inching their way along special rails attached to the mother ship's hull in the larger drawing.

# the many lives of a spaceship

Here is the 'Project Orion' pusher-plate concept for the *Discovery* spacecraft, which caused Kubrick's design team so many headaches in November 1965. The idea was eventually dropped, but many detailed drawings were made, showing the tankage and the complicated shock absorbers which would cushion the main ship from the intense energy of miniaturized nuclear explosions at the rear.

Only the Cold War-crazy world of the 1960s could have dreamed up such an idea. Today, it seems vaguely preposterous, not to say extremely dangerous. Currently, all nuclear explosions are banned in space by international agreement.

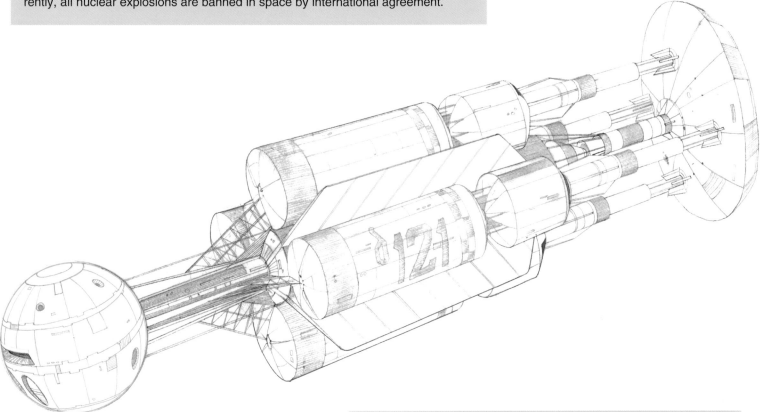

An early version, the so-called 'dragonfly' configuration (below), matches almost exactly the description of *Discovery* in Clarke's novel. The V-shaped fins are radiators, which would dissipate the excess heat generated by the nuclear engine. Eventually they were eliminated because they looked too much like wings of some kind.

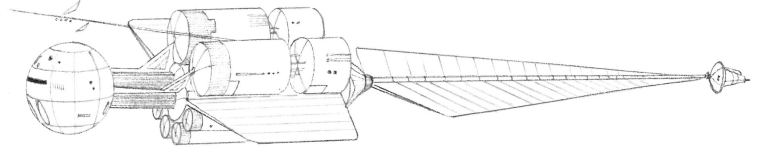

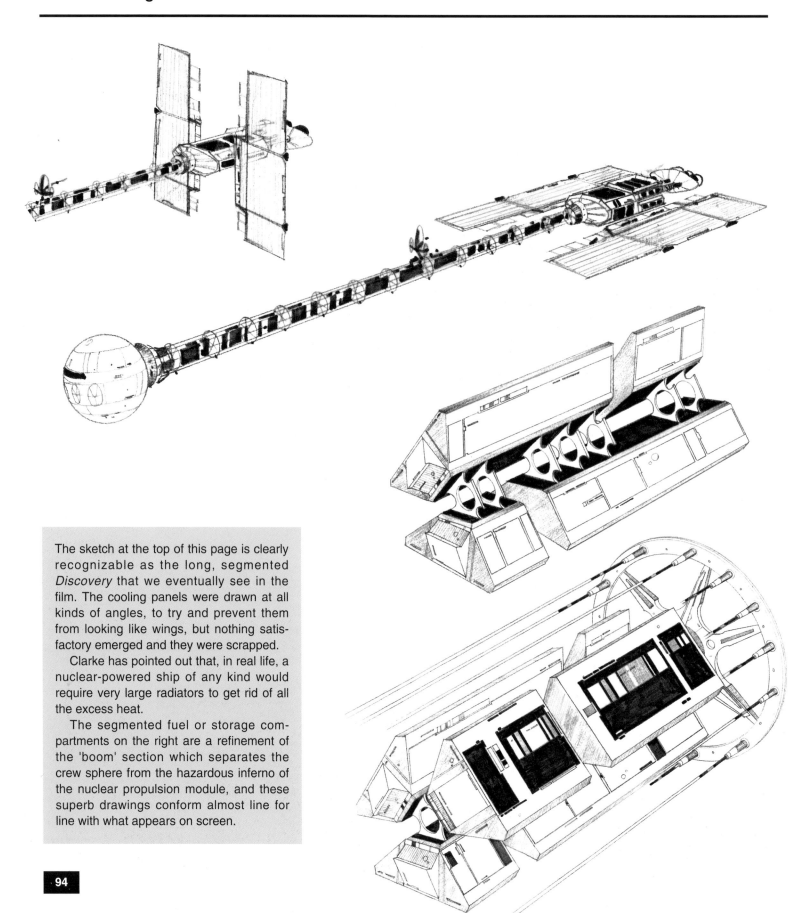

The sketch at the top of this page is clearly recognizable as the long, segmented *Discovery* that we eventually see in the film. The cooling panels were drawn at all kinds of angles, to try and prevent them from looking like wings, but nothing satisfactory emerged and they were scrapped.

Clarke has pointed out that, in real life, a nuclear-powered ship of any kind would require very large radiators to get rid of all the excess heat.

The segmented fuel or storage compartments on the right are a refinement of the 'boom' section which separates the crew sphere from the hazardous inferno of the nuclear propulsion module, and these superb drawings conform almost line for line with what appears on screen.

**Mock-up:**
*A test photograph of the 'dragonfly' version of the Jupiter spaceship, carved out of poly-styrene and roughly painted.*

**Stanley's rocket boffins:**
*Fred Ordway (above, left) and Harry Lange look purposeful in the pod bay set.*

with a particular obstacle: even though he was a skilled artist, he didn't belong to any of the right cinematographic unions.

Kubrick side-stepped the whole mess by applying his usual dose of crisp logic to the problem and appointed Lange as a technical consultant, for which union membership was not required. By the time *2001* was released, Lange had been working on the set for so long he was able to gain acceptance into the industry and share formal credit with Masters and Archer for production design.

In Lange, Kubrick had found the highly informed imagination he needed: 'Good illustrators are a dime a dozen,' he said flatly to a startled Lange at their first interview, 'but illustrators who know about spaceflight systems? Now, *that's* a combination I can use.'

Lange got his own back by saying he'd only stay on in New York if Kubrick paid him a lot of money. So Kubrick paid him a lot of money; and nobody even *mentioned* three years in London at first, nor suggested to Lange that he'd end up—just like Kubrick—living in Britain for good.

With Ordway providing reams of paperwork and material gathered from sources right across the US manufacturing base, Lange mapped out the spaceships, control panels, suits and moonbases during an intense six months in New York, from February up until June 1965, after which he turned several of the main ideas into fully developed technical drawings.

Then the entire production moved across the Atlantic to England.

Just as well, because the Polaris offices on Central Park West were getting pretty crowded. Kubrick's assistant Ray Lovejoy had arrived from London, along with executive producer Victor Lyndon; Roger Caras was gearing up for his lengthy publicity campaign (he'd just quit Columbia after ten years' service in order to join the *2001* team) and various artists and draughtsmen were also on hand, as Tony Masters' creative empire expanded. Artists Richard McKenna and Roy Carnon were already churning out colour pre-production artwork. Later on, space artist Robert McCall would come on board and create his memorable series of publicity illustrations: in particular, his famous space station poster.

of creative forces in the chaos of a huge film production. His style of command involved great helpings of patience and kindness. Since 1946 he had worked on dozens of films, most notably with John Box on David Lean's *Lawrence of Arabia*, another of MGM's more famous products. Masters took command of the art direction as a whole, particularly the planning of the control decks, passenger compartments, pod bays and so forth. The eerie hotel room at the film's climax was his work. In terms of set design, *2001* was Tony's film—perhaps the greatest achievement of his long and distinguished career. He was ably assisted by John Hoesli, who helped to manage the day-to-day nightmare of set construction and prop-making. (Eventually, thirty draughtsmen would be kept in harness at Borehamwood for more than a year, drawing up thousands of construction plans.) Ernie Archer joined the crew soon afterwards, and created the spectacular African landscape illusions for the film's opening sequences.

Working under Masters, Harry Lange produced hundreds of spaceship and hardware drawings and contributed to every aspect of the film's design—though it's worth stressing that, for all his talent, Lange started out as a babe-in-the-woods as far as film work was concerned. He was an aerospace expert, not a movie man. *2001* was something of an accelerated learning programme for him. In fact, Lange's lack of specific film-making experience presented him

By the end of June 1965 most of the crew had transferred to the giant MGM production facility in Borehamwood, north London. Kubrick stayed on in America for another couple of months, and Ordway tied up the remaining schedule of consultancy deals until early August, but by the end of that summer everybody's feet were planted firmly in England. Lange and Ordway ploughed through their great swathes of material: the twenty heavy trunkloads of data which they had shipped over on the *S.S. France*. The special effects teams began gearing up for their long months in harness under the direction of Wally Veevers, Con Pedersen, and MGM's in-house expert Tom Howard. (Wally Gentleman was on hand for a while, but retired early with an illness. He wasn't very complementary about *2001* in subsequent interviews.) Kubrick also hired a very young and enthusiastic Canadian lad called Douglas Trumbull to do a few bits and pieces of artwork.

Tony Masters supervised as the first of the many impressive interior sets started rising up from the studio floors. Harry Lange set about translating the ideas he had come up with into models that could be photographed convincingly. The set designers needed to know very urgently what the *exteriors* were supposed to look like, so that live-action photography would tie in smoothly. There was a constant interchange of information between all the various departments. Plenty of lively lunchtime meetings resulted from the often complicated business of getting everyone working in the same direction. All kinds of animated discussions would break out about the realism or relevance of this or that design, so that even Kubrick, that stickler for authenticity, was occasionally to be heard reminding his overheated experts that this wasn't real—it was only a *movie*.

Lange assembled a team of modelmakers and began the difficult business of turning his drawings into convincing three-dimensional objects. The principal challenge was that the models had to be super-detailed. Kubrick wanted to be able to shoot them from all interesting angles, at all scales and speeds, so that he could choose the best sequences later on during the editing process. Consequently, he demanded that the models look perfect, no matter how close the camera came. In response, Lange decided to use plastic kit components for fine detailing on engines, or in little nooks and crannies.

This might all seem familiar stuff today, but *2001*'s Lego-like space vehicles were a far cry from the smooth-skinned rocketships of previous science fiction movies. NASA was testing its spidery lunar modules, whose appearance was utterly unlike any kind of fantasy rocket vehicle, with no streamlining, all struts and beams and asymmetrical boxes. Clearly, real-life spaceships weren't going to be pointy cigar-shaped darts with fins on the back. To keep pace with these changes in technology, a new kind of movie spaceship was required. With no need for heavy heatshields or atmospheric streamlining, a true ship of space would have a lightweight construction, with few concessions to grace or beauty. The Jupiter vehicle *Discovery* reflects this. She's all modules and clip-together components and is quite clearly incapable of flying through the air or landing on any planet. Her spine, a long, segmented boom of fuel or storage tanks, is painfully thin. She'd snap in half under her own weight under Earth gravity.

Lange was faced with the complexity of his own designs. Each spaceship would be an amalgam of dozens of weirdly shaped components, but *repetitive* shapes would be a common feature: rocket nozzles, fuel tanks, landing legs and so on. Model kits provided a handy way of repeating the small details consistently. Today, every sci-fi movie maker reaches for the nearest Airfix kit. In 1966, with the arguable exception of Gerry and Sylvia Anderson's *Thunderbirds* on TV, this was all new territory.

As a matter of fact, Kubrick did make an approach to the Andersons. Sylvia remembers getting a phone call from Kubrick inviting her for lunch:

'Fine,' she said, 'but I hope you're not going to ask for any of our special effects people?'

'Oh well, in which case there's no point in having lunch,' said Kubrick, and promptly put the phone down.

Sylvia found this abrupt behaviour rather impolite, but those who know Kubrick will tell

**Designer-in-Chief:**
*Tony Masters in 1967.*

you that this was just his way of preventing an afternoon going to waste when there was plenty of work to be getting on with. His various production departments managed, nevertheless, to persuade plenty of modelmakers and technicians to defect from the *Thunderbirds* camp.

But the model kits they made so much use of were no cop-out solution. Basic hulls for the vehicles were hand-crafted in wood and fibreglass or custom-moulded plastic. Certain elements had to be fabricated in what amounted to a factory environment: in particular, the *Discovery*'s three massive propulsion housings, her six exhaust nozzles and thirty-odd storage modules (divided among ten vertebrated boom segments) and her nuclear power module with its mass of tiny pipes and gizmos. These separate units were produced with careful attention to consistent detailing. Here in particular, imaginative cannibalization of model kits proved very helpful.

The command module sphere at the front of *Discovery* was a fibreglass ball six feet in diameter. Another plastic sphere was moulded with a diameter that was wider by just fractions of an inch. From this thin-skinned ball, strips were cut to provide a layer of stick-on 'panels' for the fibreglass shell. Extra detailing was provided by metal foils and adhesive papers with varying textures. The main model ended up 54 feet long. A smaller model for long-shots came in at a still impressive 15 feet.

The rotating space station owed its shape to the most serious proposals made by Lange's illustrious colleague and friend at NASA, Wernher von Braun. Lange and Kubrick agreed on the famous two-wheel shape so that the rear part of the station could be seen as if still under construction by space workers, with ribs and girders exposed. The eight-foot-diameter model was stuffed full of tiny lightbulbs which glowed behind all the windows of the station's front wheel. There were no fibre optics or LEDs in those days. As often as not, shooting would be interrupted when heat from all the tiny elements threatened to melt and buckle the structure.

The three-foot-diameter *Aries* lunar shuttle vehicle had motorized legs which extended as it came in to land. (Ordway, Caras and others made a special trip to the Grumman plant at

Bethpage, New York, to see the emerging Lunar Module's legs under construction.) Compressed air jets in the exhaust nozzles kicked up dust on touchdown, to convincing effect.

At the height of all this construction effort, 103 modelmakers were employed on various projects. They came from all kinds of specialist disciplines. There were boat builders, architectural students, fine artists, sculptors, lithographers, metalworkers, and even some ivory carvers fresh off a whaling boat. This minor army was employed largely on a freelance basis on short-term contracts. Turn-over was high, as more and more of them failed to satisfy the exacting demands of the production's seniors. The only ones who stood the course were the extremely skilled perfectionists, all of whom had to possess the additional quality of being immune to the shocks and disappointments of suddenly having to scrap several weeks' worth of work and start again. This happened quite frequently: the designs were often being altered right up until the very last moment before the models were set in front of the cameras.

Full-size space pods, pressure suits and helmets required the services of independent industrial companies. The suits were manufactured by a well-respected Manchester firm, Frankenstein (Air and Sea Rescue, Division of). The helmets were moulded by a London company, Master Models, along with chest packs and several spacecraft inner shells. The British Hawker Siddeley aircraft company produced pod interiors and instrument layouts to specifications that were so exacting, they might just as well have been working on a genuine aerospace contract. Hawker's team leader Arthur Cole remembers:

*We were contracted to provide consultancy during the early stages of production, and our responsibility was communications systems, voice, video, radar, navigation and control systems, attitude and orbit, remote manipulators and so on. Between us we derived many instrument layouts and provided advice on the likely shape of various structural features such as antennas, propulsion and control jets, and relevant hatch and docking systems.*

Kubrick believed that if *2001* was to be credible on a technical level, then no detail was

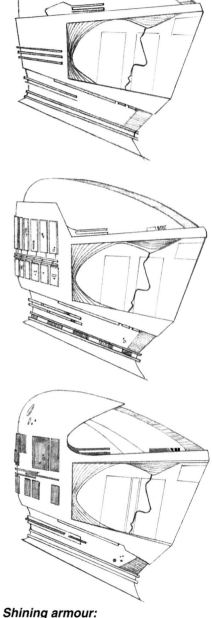

**Shining armour:**
*The profiles of Lange's unusual helmet designs (above) may have originated from the deerstalkers and cloth caps he so favoured. Panels at the back represented plug-in computer modules, which were tailored for specific missions or spacewalks.*

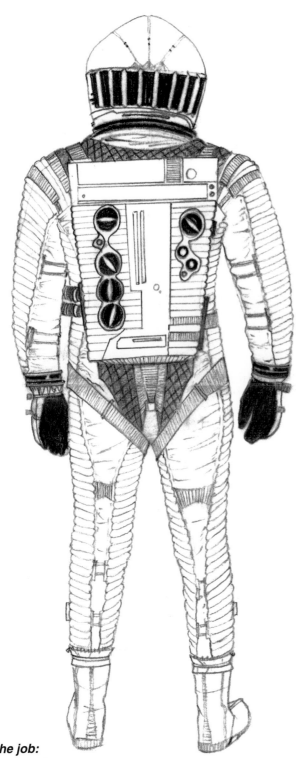

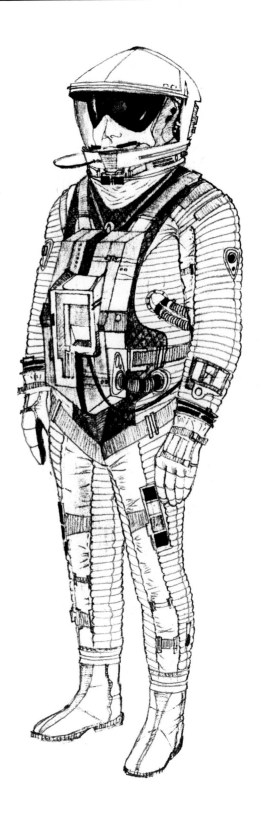

**Suited for the job:**
Lange's spacesuit ideas
made their way almost
unaltered onto the screen.

***The trench:***
*This highly developed drawing of the below-surface section of the lunar base landing area shows the spherical passenger ship being lowered on a hydraulic platform. The darkened areas on the left and right side walls are eventually to become recesses for 'matting' window action of the base's crew at work. Those sequences would be live action, scaled down photographically and later combined with footage of the trench (a model about twelve feet deep).*

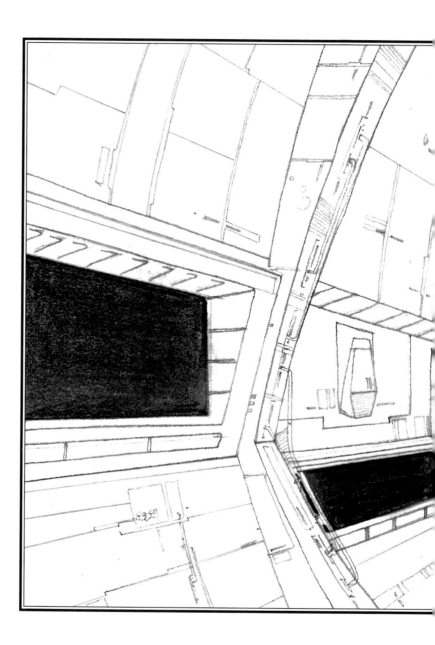

# a thriving underground city on the moon... by when?

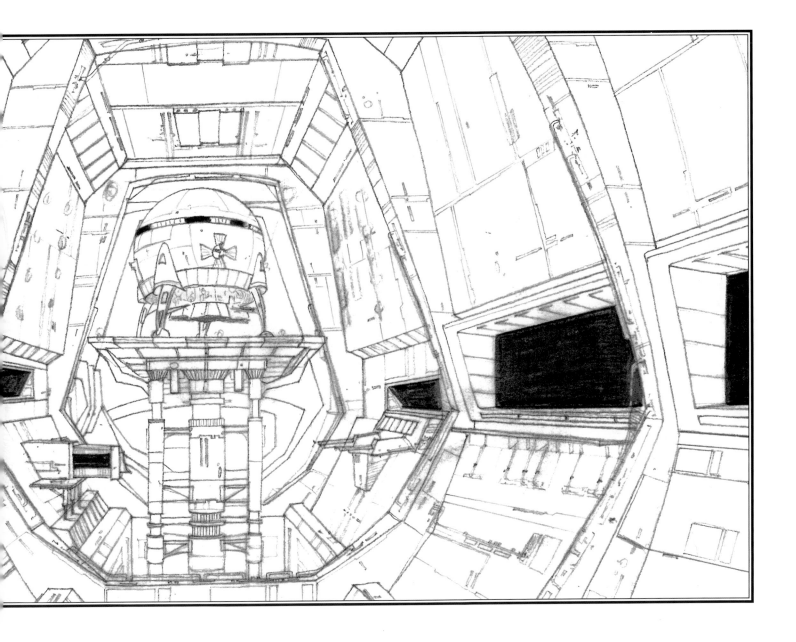

This vision of a giant underground moonbase is perhaps the most futuristic *and* the most out-dated concept in Kubrick's *2001: A Space Odyssey*. The political and financial commitment that would be required to build such a place will remain beyond the reach of terrestrial governments for some time to come. Only a vast international effort would make it possible. At least, that's the common wisdom at the moment.

But the future is always full of surprises. Eager dreamers of the *Apollo* era ('blue sky thinkers', the NASA administrators used to call them) may have been sadly surprised that moonbases like this never made it off the drawing boards. Perhaps our generation may be equally surprised by some new technology, some urgent and unexpected financial or social motivation, that boosts us back to the moon after all.

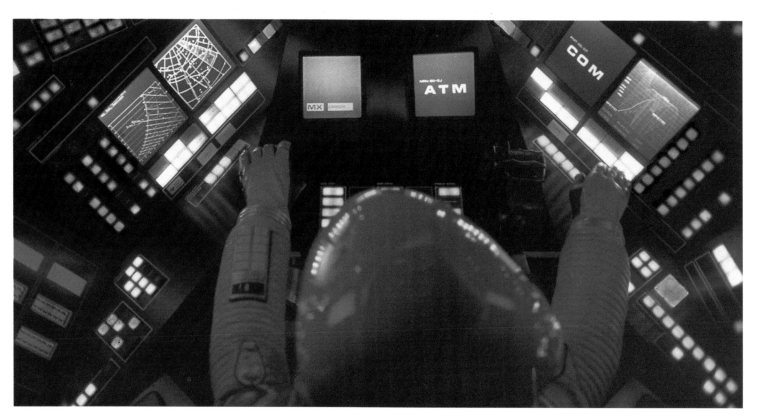

**Inside and out:**
*The elaborate interior of
a space pod (above).*

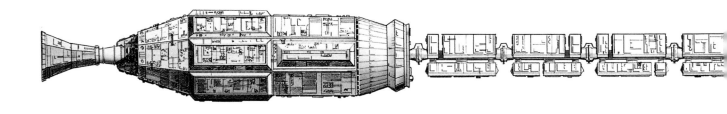

**The command module:**
*The spherical crew cabin takes shape (above and right) with detailing provided by thin metal foils and subtle variations of paint finish.*

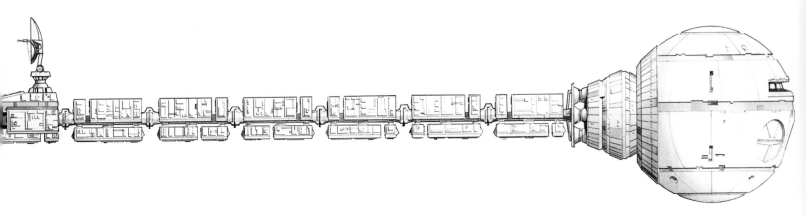

The spaceship *Discovery* as it appears in the film. The wire frame around the fuel and storage modules in the long boom was stripped away, making the already slender vehicle appear even more fragile. Lange says that the ship's similarity to a bleached, vertebrated dinosaur skeleton was deliberate.

too small to consider. Of course there was the entirely separate problem of whether or not this mass of engineering input could ensure the movie's *historical* plausibility. As we shall see, the world outside Kubrick's studio was changing in ways too complex and subtle to be analysed by even the cleverest Hawker Siddeley expert.

For all her magnificent astronautical realism, *Discovery*'s true-life equivalents couldn't expect to be in operation as soon as the year 2001; and by 1967 this was already becoming evident to some observers of the space business, as the US Congress began for the first time to slash at NASA's budget with a vengeance. However, the optimism of Kubrick's technologists seemed unquenchable. Perhaps, like their counterparts at Cape Kennedy, they were just *too busy* in their intense and closed-off little world to notice Vietnam, Martin Luther King, LSD, the Counter-Culture...?

Fred Ordway might already have sensed the way NASA's future was going. After 1967 his career was dominated by the energy business: nuclear waste management, synthetic and alcohol-based fuels, environmental studies: very urgent but very terrestrial concerns. (Today he is renowned as a space *historian*, which is an interesting shift of emphasis.)

That September of 1965 though, Ordway's problem on *2001* was the sheer volume of data streaming in from companies like Hawker and its giant American cousins. He was caught in the middle, between Kubrick's ceaseless demands for up-to-the-minute realism and the growing urgency of the production schedule. Everybody was scrabbling to get things ready for the start of main filming by the turn of that year, and all departments were stretched to their very limits.

Suddenly, Kubrick and Clarke decided over a cosy dinner that it might be nice for *Discovery* to go to Saturn instead of Jupiter, so that the planet's ring system could be shown, and Ordway was instructed to come up with a detailed memo outlining current knowledge about Saturn. Clarke loved this new idea so much that he retained Saturn as the destination planet in his novel. He wanted to demonstrate the 'perturbation' manoeuvre, whereby the spacecraft would use Jupiter's gravitational field to fling it towards Saturn. Kubrick, for his part, was keen

on the rings. So it was agreed. *Discovery* would go to Saturn. But the special effects department was horrified, and spent several tense weeks getting this decision reversed. They'd already spent three hectic months preparing for a visit to Jupiter, and were up against deadline on dozens of different aspects of the movie. They were alarmed at the prospect of having to throw in a Saturnian ring system at short notice (though Trumbull, perhaps pursuing 'unfinished business', did just that in his own film, *Silent Running*, in 1972). Lange's team narrowly avoided having to reconfigure *Discovery* yet again. A new mission profile might have involved different engines, fuel pods and so on. Just for once, Kubrick *wasn't* going to get his way.

Or was he? At the end of October, Kubrick became fascinated by a research project called *Orion*, being undertaken by the physicist Freeman Dyson (from Princeton's Institute of Advanced Studies) which involved powering a spaceship with pulsed energy from miniaturized nuclear explosions. A giant buffer plate would smooth out the shocks. Models a few feet long were already being launched a few feet into the air using conventional explosives. Eventually a nuclear treaty would ban the use of such systems; but just then, Kubrick loved the idea that *bombs* should power us to the stars. So *Discovery* was redesigned. Then Kubrick worried, probably quite rightly, that a bomb-driven ship might make too many people think about *Dr Strangelove*, and anyway, the idea of a spaceship put-put-putting its way across the solar system seemed rather too comical. The re-design was cancelled. (Project *Orion*'s memory survives: the spaceplane bears that name.)

By December 1965, only days away from the start of principal photography, Ordway was frustrated enough to write in his diary:

*We are continually facing difficulties of decision-making... Whatever US industry comes up with doesn't always please Stanley... Many design aspects of the vehicles for the film change so regularly that it becomes impossible at times to finalize anything... The screenplay has a decided tendency to change rather rapidly, even as we are moving forward... Film experts tell me this is highly unorthodox and produces more difficulties than necessary.*

Then there was the occasion when Clarke and Kubrick took a look at the *Orion* flight deck set, and Clarke remarked in passing that it reminded him slightly of a Chinese restaurant. 'That kills it for me,' Kubrick said, and ordered an immediate redesign of the set. Clarke jotted a chastened note in his diary that he 'must keep away from the Art Department for a few days'.

The search for perfection was merciless. Mr H.R. Premaratne was a talented engineer and Clarke's personal assistant at the time. Like many people who worked on the production, he regards his *2001* experience as having been a real adventure, and something to be proud of. But there were obviously some difficult times during the long struggle to get things right:

*I well remember the number of times we detailed the 'Discovery' command module, when Mr Kubrick would come along and, after a critical examination, would order scrapping the whole thing and re-doing it, this time using more convincing materials. Of course we worked under Harry [Lange]'s direction, and when we finally finished the whole thing, giving it a metallic finish using grained silver adhesive paper, complete with details, it was given a coat of paint obliterating all the metallic effect.*

One can surmise that this rethink was the result of NASA's increasing use of ceramics, resins and exotic compounds on their space vehicles. The polished steel skins of traditional sci-fi spaceships were gone forever. But the consequence of all this heartbreaking effort was that *Discovery* would still look convincing thirty years later. (Incidentally, Mr Premaratne went on to become Sri Lanka's ambassador to Burma. Clarke has wondered which he might have found more difficult: international diplomacy, or working for Stanley Kubrick.)

By and large, of course, everybody was having the time of their lives. The difficulties only added to the fun. And love him or hate him *at the time*, many voices today will testify to Kubrick's perfectionism as the driving engine of their own best work.

The final product of nearly three years' intense effort at Borehamwood was the most realistic space fiction film ever made, bar none. By any standards, *2001* still looks convincing today. In the 1960s, of course, there'd never

been anything like it. Senior NASA *Apollo* administrator George Mueller paid a visit to the studios, along with astronaut chief Deke Slayton, and was light-heartedly shocked by all the hardware and detailed documentation piling up everywhere. Mueller dubbed Kubrick's empire 'NASA East'. Slayton is said to have remarked, 'You must've been conned by a used-capsule salesman.'

Obviously this not-so-fantastical project was getting things more or less right. Except, maybe, for one thing: a visiting Soviet dignitary, after expressing guarded enthusiasm, looked at all the control panels and said, without the slightest trace of a smile: 'Of course, you know all these instructions should be in Russian?'

The *alien* artifacts, however, proved to be even more of a problem than the terrestrial spaceships. Black monoliths were easy enough to describe on paper, but not so easy to film convincingly. Chunks of rock were cut, polished and photographed—only to end up looking like useless chunks of rock. That extra 'something' was missing. Painted wooden and plastic structures showed up every warp and flaw under the lights. Matted artwork also failed.

At last a credible technique was devised by which a blacker-than-black finish could be produced on a truly smooth surface. A heavy wooden monolith was sanded, rubbed, sanded again. Then a mixture of black paint and pencil graphite was applied—and rubbed down, applied and rubbed down, over and over, till the slab glowed with an eerie blackness. It shone like silk, yet sucked up light like a black hole. It had a surface texture like nothing on Earth (after all, pencil graphite is not a common element of everyday paint finishes).

Touching this immaculate surface on set with greasy fingers was proclaimed a capital offence. Between scenes, the twelve-foot-high artifact, with its sensitive skin, was swaddled in thick layers of plastic sheeting and cotton wool. Many months would separate its starring performances: in the little clearing outside the apemen's cave; in its trench several metres below the lunar surface; and finally in the dazzling white hotel room. (The slab floating in space above Jupiter was a 'miniature'.)

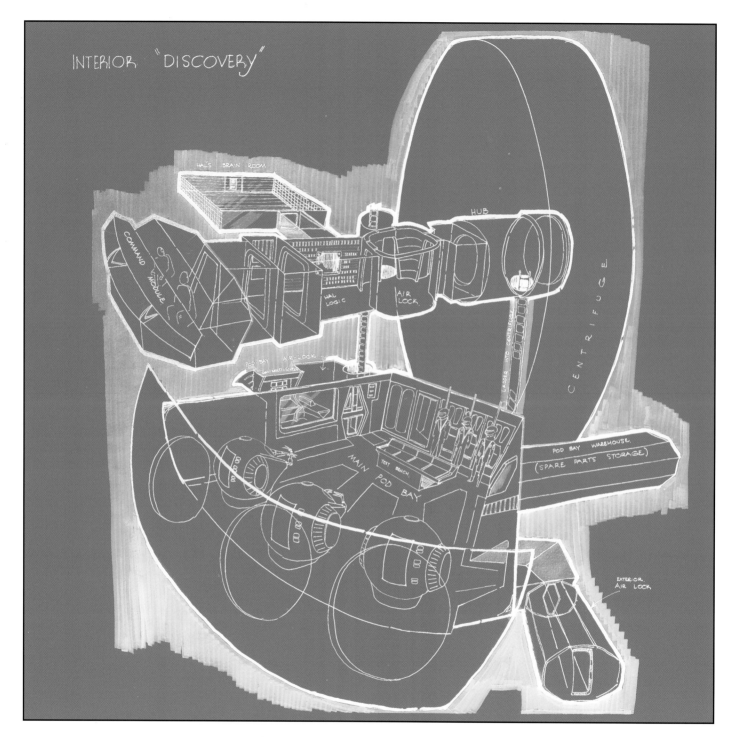

INTERIOR "DISCOVERY"

HALS BRAIN ROOM

COMMAND MODULE

HAL LOGIC

AIR LOCK

HUB

CENTRIFUGE

LADDER INTO CENTRIFUGE

POD BAY AIR-LOCK

MAIN POD BAY

TEST BENCH

POD BAY WAREHOUSE. (SPARE PARTS STORAGE)

EXTERIOR AIR LOCK

***Inner spaces:***
*This blueprint shows the supposed interior layout of the Jupiter spaceship's crew quarters.*

**The grand illusion:**
*Making the control deck on
screen was a tricky business.
The exterior of the set looked
far less ordered than its cool
and futuristic interior (right).
The set plan at the bottom of
this page features a slanted
mirror, so that actors Dullea
and Lockwood could be
photographed at suitably
unearthly angles.*

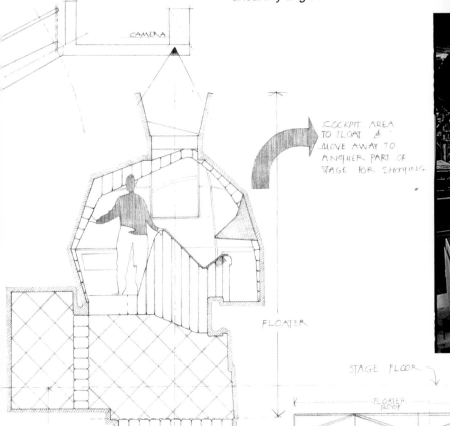

CAMERA

COCKPIT AREA
TO FLOAT &
MOVE AWAY TO
ANOTHER PART OF
STAGE FOR SHOOTING

FLOATER

STAGE FLOOR

FLOATER
ROOF

FLOATER
ROOF

CAMERA

FLOATER
MIRROR

FLOATER

TANK 10-8¾"

3'-3" CAMERA
ROSTRUM

FLOOR OF STAGE TANK

Kubrick had wanted to be even more ambitious than this. He had wanted shimmering multi-faceted pictures to appear, deep within a transparent crystalline pillar, as though it was literally showing its primitive pupils the way to a better life. Today, advertisers and movie-makers regularly make use of computer-generated fractal surfaces, glassy reflections and so forth. Kubrick had none of these toys to play with. He decided to experiment by projecting images into slabs of clear perspex, trying to make use of internal reflections. At great expense, a very large and precise block of 'Lucite' was moulded by an outside contractor and brought on stage. The newspapers heralded it, probably correctly,

as the largest and most precise casting of transparent plastic the world had ever seen. Unfortunately it wasn't optically pure enough to provide the required effect. The perspex experiment was abandoned, very much to the disappointment of the block's all-too terrestrial manufacturers.

And so it was that a featureless black rectangular box managed to persuade us that we were looking at a sophisticated mechanism from another world. It was the boldest of *2001*'s rich array of illusions. The simplicity of the image, born out of countless experimental failures with more complex ideas, turned out to be just right.

*Dining in:*
*The food preparation area in the Jupiter spacecraft (right) was designed by RCA Whirlpool. Kubrick subverted the sales job by showing astronaut Bowman burning his fingers on an overheated tray. The Bell Telephone Company created a videophone (lower right), with instructions, which Kubrick used to suggest the banality of communications in the year 2001.*

Kubrick ordered many designs for orbiting nuclear weapon platforms from Lange and Masters. This drawing shows a version that actually made it to the shooting stage, as one of the first spaceships that appears on screen. Anxious to avoid too many associations with *Dr Strangelove*, however, Kubrick decided not to make it so obvious in his film that this expensive and delicate artifact of space was a war machine.

Clarke's novel mentions the bombs specifically, and the final chapter contains what some readers have seen as an ambiguous description of the Starchild detonating the orbiting bombs because of his preference for 'a cleaner sky'.

## INSTRUCTIONS FOR USE OF VISIONPHONE

**1** If you do not know the number see INFORMATION instructions

**2** If you do know your number, proceed as follows

**3** Press 2626 if you want a vision connection
Press 2627 if you want a non-vision connection

**4** Press ON button to initiate your call

**5** Press CALL to place the video system into operation

**6** To see yourself prior to composing your number, press SELF

**7** If you desire to see the person you are calling but not be seen yourself, press 1 WAY · Otherwise, press 2 WAY for vision at both ends. *Note:* the person you are phoning can override your request for vision.

**8** The screen will now indicate READY FOR CALL

**9** You should promptly compose your number on the touchtone panel directly below. You may start talking when the words CHANNEL OPEN appear on the screen.

**10** You can hold your channel open by pressing the HOLD button and you can speak through the intercom by pressing LOC Compose intercom numbers on the touchtone.

**11** At the end of your conversation the words CHANNEL CLOSED and the cost of your call will be indicated on the screen. You may either insert your credit card through the indicated slot near the bottom of the panel or place into the slots the appropriate coins. 50, 75 and 100 cent pieces only are accepted.

## INFORMATION INSTRUCTIONS

**1** To obtain a number unknown to you, press the INFORMATION button to the left above the pad.

**2** Compose on the alphabetical panel above the pad the first two letters of the continent (for example, Eu for Europe,) then the name of the major political subdivision (state, Province, etc.), and finally the city or town. What you have composed will be confirmed on the screen.

**3** Now compose on the alphabetical panel the name of the individual or company you desire to phone. The appropriate section of the local directory will be displayed on the screen.

**4** The specific portion of the directory section will be displayed on the screen with yellow shading over the names being searched, for example WINDSOR.

**5** When you have found your number press the INFORMATION button again to deactivate the channel.

**6** Proceed to make your call according to the instructions at the left.

INFORMATION

# 5: the flight simulators

THE LUNAR EXCAVATION sequences were filmed during a hectic week just after Christmas 1965. Kubrick built this particular set on a large stage at Shepperton. Borehamwood wasn't large enough to cope with what he had in mind: a huge trench incorporating 90 tons of carefully graded, washed and coloured sand. By January 8, 1966 he and his camera crew were back in north London, because another film production needed to move into Shepperton. Shooting of the space station interiors and the lunar scientists in their underground conference room was completed at Borehamwood over the next month, then actors Keir Dullea and Gary Lockwood remained on call from February up to the end of August, for the *Discovery* interior scenes.

So, by the autumn of 1966, the principal actors had sloughed off their spacesuits and disappeared. Some of them would be back in harness again later for their arduous and repetitive publicity tours. The apeman scenes were completed in mid-1967, with dancers and mime artists wearing the heavy costumes. Meanwhile, throughout 1966, the special effects team had been getting on with business—and they still had another year's work ahead of them.

Victor Lyndon's pre-production notes, assembled in May 1965, run to 160 pages and specify the live-action photography in exact detail, including the construction of the centrifuge; but the hefty document becomes a

little vague as far as the outer space scenes are concerned. In what now seems a delicious touch of understatement, the beautiful ballet of Heywood Floyd's shuttle docking with a tumbling space station is summarized in one short paragraph, with a note that 'this is a special effects sequence with star backing.' For other scenes, Lyndon says only that 'process photography may be required.'

*2001: A Space Odyssey* may be three decades old by now, but the technical procedures used during the production were the direct forebears of the computerized methods that prevail today. Modern effects still involve the same old problem: how to combine many different elements at different scales, shot at different times, on the same final piece of film. Kubrick's elaborate space epic remains as good a primer in that art as could be wished for.

Kubrick's first recruit for the *2001* effects team was Wally Veevers, who had already worked on *Dr Strangelove*. He was a traditional craftsman, the sort of man whose dedication and ingenuity gave British technicians such a good reputation in the international film world. Next on board was Tom Howard, in charge of special effects for MGM, who had worked on several of George Pal's fantasy and SF pictures. Kubrick may have criticized the rather naïve style of such films, but he took note of the technical accomplishments. Howard won an Oscar for his work on Pal's *Tom Thumb* in 1958, and it was inevitable that MGM would expect him to play a role on *2001*. But Kubrick had also been much impressed by the work of two young Los Angeles animators, Con Pederson and Doug Trumbull.

Pederson, who had trained in animation at the University of California in Los Angeles, shared with Harry Lange a close link with rocket designer Wernher von Braun. 'I was drafted into the army in 1956, aged 22. They shipped me off to the First Armored Division in Louisiana, from which nobody was ever known to escape short of their time, but Walt Disney personally brought me to the attention of von Braun, because his rocket team had just acquired an animation camera, and they didn't know how to use it. I was attached to what used to be called the Redstone Arsenal in Huntsville, working on short animated films to show various space ideas to Congress.'

Disney was already collaborating with von Braun on an ambitious television series, *Man in Space*, and Pederson worked on various animated effects. The shows, networked across America, helped prepare the public for the creation of NASA in 1958. After release from the military, Pederson carried on working for Disney (animating Pluto the dog) before joining Graphic Films in 1959. 'I was with Graphic for six years, and I hired Doug Trumbull in 1963 to do airbrush work for animation backgrounds. He was a terrific artist, just out of school, and he fitted right in.'

In late 1963, with Trumbull's keen assistance, Pederson directed a Graphic Films project called *To The Moon and Beyond*, commissioned for the New York World's Fair. 'We made the film in about five months. It was a helluva rush. It was in 70mm format, projected onto the curved surface of a planetarium-style dome, in this theatre that they'd already built for the Fair. They didn't have anything to project, and we—foolishly, maybe—stepped into the breach. Kubrick saw the film in 1964, while it was still showing, and contacted us.'

Throughout the busy brainstorming period at Kubrick's New York office during 1964 and early 1965, Graphic Films shuttled ideas and artwork from California. 'But then Kubrick went to north London, and we were still north of Los Angeles. It was hard to work with the distance between us, so in the summer of 1965 he hired Doug and me to go over to England.'

In fact, Trumbull remembers beating Pederson to the post when it came to signing up for *2001*. 'I thought what Stanley was doing sounded great, so I called him up in England and said, "Hey, I really want to stick with this thing. Can I come over and work on it?" And he said, "Sure." I sensed this was a big opportunity for me, though when I began I had no idea where it was really going.'

Although Trumbull had started out as an illustrator, he developed an incredible cinematic expertise. In consultation with Kubrick, Pederson and Veevers, he devised many of the complex photographic systems which the film required, and the famous 'tunnel of light' at the film's climax was largely his work. In fact, there is scarcely an aspect of the film's visual construction which didn't involve him at some point, from painting star fields to detailing models. Roger Caras remembers that 'Doug Trumbull had Kubrick's greatest respect, although he was just a baby! He worked very hard, and very creatively. He was a driven young man.'

Even Trumbull was surprised at the extent of his contribution. 'I came up with a lot of ideas that I didn't expect, and that *they* didn't expect. I got my fingers in a lot of pies, and it turned out to be a terrific experience. The whole crew—we were all learning as we went along. It was like a film school for me.'

Today, Trumbull heads his own special effects company, pioneering new systems in cinematography, projection, theme park technology, animation and computerization. His work has featured in *Close Encounters of the Third Kind,* the first *Star Trek* feature film, *Blade Runner* and *Back to the Future,* not to mention his own directorial efforts, the cult space ecology movie *Silent Running* (1971) and the (less fortunate) *Brainstorm* (1985). George Lucas's Industrial Light and Magic effects company is run by Trumbull's ex-apprentices. Without his prior example, *Star Wars* would not have had the benefit of an increasingly perfected and standardized set of optical procedures.

Apart from Trumbull's and Pederson's work on *To The Moon and Beyond*, Kubrick also encountered a short documentary financed by the Canadian Film Board. *Universe* was a guided tour of the cosmos, featuring stars and galaxies created by Wally Gentleman. One day, relaxing over a cup of coffee, Gentleman noticed sunlight reflecting from the hot, swirling surface of his drink, and when he poured in some cream, the reflections created spiral-shaped patterns of light on the ceiling above him. It was a happy accident. A few seconds later and he might never have noticed it. For *Universe* he capitalized on this effect by mixing oils and paints in a vortex of fluid, and bouncing focused spotlights onto a screen, which he then photographed. For other effects he shot through various transparent liquids, with inks and paints slowly dispersing to create nebulous swirls.

Gentleman's *Universe* technique influenced several scenes during Bowman's 'trip', during which he sees stars and galaxies forming from whorls of gas and dust. (Another significant link: *Universe* was narrated by Douglas Raine, who became the voice of HAL9000.)

Other talents featured in the principal effects squad: Bryan Loftus, Jack Malick, Colin Cantwell, Bruce Logan, Frederick Martin and David Osborne. In addition, many junior *2001* technicians, uncredited at the time, have become today's special effects supremos: Brian Johnson, lured away from Gerry and Sylvia Anderson's *Thunderbirds* television show, won an Oscar creating effects for Ridley Scott's *Alien*; Zoran Perisic won his own award for making *Superman* fly, and Keith Hamshere is a sucessful photographer for the film industry.

Hamshere started out as a junior at Baron's, a high-society photographic studio in West London. In early 1966 Kubrick signed him up to photograph spacecraft models for certain effects sequences. 'If someone said, "this is your studio, you can do whatever you want, you can have all the toys you want. Now start playing," you'd think it was your dream come true. I was twenty-one years old, with an entire studio at Borehamwood, all the camera gear I needed, about five darkrooms and four people working for me. It was the happiest two years of my working life.'

The main *Discovery* spacecraft model was 54 feet long, with a command module sphere about 6 feet in diameter. This large scale provided Kubrick and the effects team with a good

**Slender profile:**
The smaller 'Discovery' model (right) was used for long shots. Here it is (below) filmed from the other side and combined with a life-size pod in such a way that the models' different scales appear properly matched.

deal of flexibility. The camera could sweep in close, or skitter off (at four feet per hour) into the distance, with no loss of detail or credibility. It could trail seemingly endlessly over *Discovery*'s enormous length, forcing the audience to conclude that they really were looking at something very big indeed. There was also the problem of playing off the pods against their mother ship, and of putting action into the control deck windows. A reasonable amount of surface area was available for incorporating window action, for hiding the machinery that opened and closed the pod bay doors, and so on. Veevers was responsible for this kind of rigging. He didn't have to range too far for most of his mechanical

components. In the last days of the old studio system, MGM maintained a crew of engineering machinists on permanent stand-by within the Borehamwood lot.

*Discovery* was rigidly supported on steel stilts, which in turn were secured to heavy foundations. Never was there a less mobile spaceship. The camera did all the moving. Alongside the intricate model ran a kind of mini railway, consisting of tracks about 150 feet long, with a camera platform mounted on them, although the platform's motion along the rails would have been almost imperceptible to the casual observer; it was pushed along by worm gearing, with excruciating slowness. Heavy

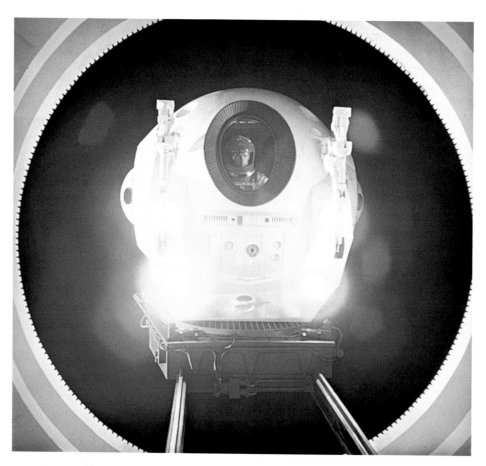

**Front window:**

*Full-scale space pods were photographed with Dullea or Lockwood inside them, clearly visible through the windows. However, in the final cut of the film, the pods are always seen with darkened windows. It was not possible to match the live-action window scenes with the twists and turns of the smaller pod miniatures. Eliminating the window views enabled Kubrick to cut more easily between full-scale and miniature shots of the pods.*

gearing devices reduced all movements to infinitesimal levels, so that watching a shoot gave the impression that nothing much was really happening. Kubrick described the process as 'like watching the hour hand of a clock.'

The camera had to run smoothly along the rails, so that when the resulting footage was projected it would show *Discovery* gliding rather than shuddering across the screen. Because the camera motion was barely visible to human observers, the occasional jiggle didn't show up until the day's shooting was over and the film processed. It was a painful business. Why was it all so *slow*? Mainly because of the inflexible limitations of films and camera lenses. *Discovery* demanded deep-focus photography in order to remain sharp from one end to the other. Lenses had to be stopped down all the way, so that their apertures were little more than the size of a pinhole. This kept the focus sharp along the model's entire length, but the light levels filtering through the lenses and onto the film were

reduced almost to insignificance. Consequently, exposure times were often several seconds per frame, rather than the more usual fiftieth of a second for live-action photography.

Every quarter-inch that the camera moved along the worm gearing had to be matched by an exact number of film frames exposed. If the mechanical gearing and the camera's frame rate fell out of phase, *Discovery*'s apparent rate of movement across screen would look shaky in the processed footage. There needed to be some kind of communication between the motor that was driving the camera along the worm gearing, and the other motors that were firing the shutter and advancing the film onto new frames. 'Selsyn' ('Self-synchronizing') electric motors were able to count the revolutions that they went through. The effects team built a system that could integrate the camera motors with the worm gearing motors by allowing them to cross-talk using analogue electrical signals. The modern art of 'motion control' was born on the *2001* model stages. Today, an inexpensive desktop digital computer decides what the motors in a motion control system should do, and sends out instructions accordingly. Back in 1966 there were no such computers available.

Illumination for the *Discovery* was provided by a concentrated bank of lighting at the far end of the shooting stage, in imitation of the dwindling sun. In deep space, shadows would be blacker than black. Ships would appear only as slivers of highlight, the rest of their bulk merely shadows blotting out the stars as they passed by. *2001*'s concession to visual storytelling was to fill in the shadow areas of its spaceships with low-level light reflected softly from the main set of lamps. The darkness of deep space as a whole, however, was not negotiable. The special effects shooting studios were swathed in black velvet, which absorbed all excess light.

Stars were painted as artwork on black backing boards—sometimes by flicking paint with a toothbrush—and then photographed on animation stands, ready to be combined with the spacecraft footage. Some of the seemingly vast star backgrounds were panels of artwork just a few feet across, photographed up close. But it wasn't possible simply to double-expose the spacecraft onto an already photographed star field. Some way had to be found of switching the stars on and off as the vehicles slid past them. If so much as one star had showed through the skin of a spacecraft, the illusion of travelling in deep space would have

been shattered. The solution adopted by the *2001* optical department was painstaking. First, the vehicles were filmed and the results processed. Then teams of young art students working at dozens of photographic enlargers were assigned a few feet of film each. They projected an enlarged image of each frame onto sheets of transparent acetate and filled in the vehicle outlines with black ink, after which the

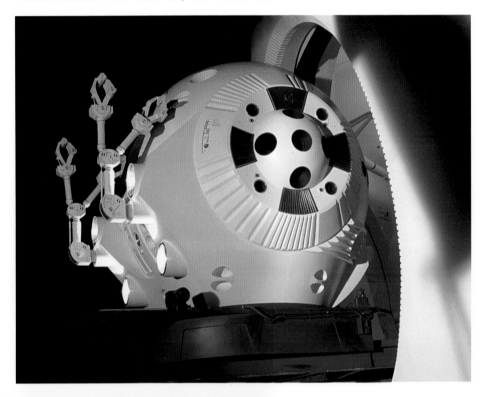

***Mother ship and pod:***
*A section of the 'Discovery' command module sphere was built full-scale (above), so that a full-sized pod could emerge from the hatch. These shots were integrated seamlessly with the smaller models (left).*

acetate sheets were gathered together and photographed, one by one, on an animation stand. The result was a 'cartoon' of black spacecraft silhouettes moving against a pure white background.

Next, the star field artwork was printed onto new film, using a camera adapted to handle the thickness of two strips of film at once: the processed cartoon mask footage on top, and unexposed film underneath. A light shone through the lens to make the new exposure. Stars blocked by the masks never registered on the fresh film underneath. So now there was a sequence of sorts: black spaceship-shaped holes, drifting across stars, turning the little points of light on and off as they passed. But this latest bit of film wasn't processed yet…

Shooting something pitch black means the film 'sees' nothing, and remains chemically unaffected, at least until processing. The moving black shapes were still waiting to be occupied by some kind of image, even though the star field had already imprinted itself around them. Now the original footage of the spaceships could be copied onto the black shapes that were waiting for them. Of course, they fitted perfectly into their own shadows. The animated silhouettes, the so-called 'mattes', were like holes through which the spaceship images could be dropped into the star background. Because the inked-in acetate silhouettes were created using the same spaceship sequences they had been traced from in the first place, every twist and turn of the space vehicles was accounted for perfectly.

Two dozen young artists, nicknamed 'the blobbers', were recruited to trace and fill in the mattes. Johnson was horrified by their working conditions. 'The black paint they used had to be fast-drying, so it was alcohol-based. The fumes were terrible. A lot of the blobbers got dizzy, or came out with headaches. A few of them got high. I wouldn't have wanted to be a blobber.'

According to Doug Trumbull's detailed account of the matte work, in the June 1968 edition of American Cinematographer, the use of hand-painted mattes was just one of a long series of carefully worked-out processes adopted by the effects team. Zoran Perisic, who slaved away on the starfield artwork with an animation camera, remembers the process as slightly less well-organized than it might have been. According to him, the best way of creating a matte would have been to shoot the spacecraft models against the black velvet, then bring the camera back to its starting position, load another roll of film, and shoot the models again—this time in silhouette, against a pure white background. 'It would have created the same mattes on an otherwise completely transparent strip of film, and we could have saved all that business with hand-painting them for every frame. Wally shot the models against black velvet, but he never shot them against white.'

In American Cinematographer, Trumbull wrote that the hand-painting of the mattes, although laborious, 'required only the simplest darkroom enlargers, and this freed up expensive animation cameras for other work'. That may be a slight tidying-up of history after the fact. For many weeks, crucial footage of the Discovery and other models against their black velvet backing lay as undeveloped 'held' takes, while the effects department tried to work out how to put the stars in.

During late 1966 it seems that Veevers thought he could create a starfield from thin sheets of steel, painted black and punctured with needlepoint holes illuminated from the rear. By placing these sheets behind the models, Veevers hoped to shoot the spacecraft and their stars all in one pass. The results were not a success. Hamshere recalls 'Every time you changed the camera lens, or the distance between it and the model, the stars looked a different size, or even went out of focus.'

Would it have been easier to create the mattes by shooting the models against a white background, as Perisic suggests? Pederson says 'It wasn't that Wally deliberately failed to shoot the models against white. He thought about it, but in those days, he couldn't be sure of duplicating the separate camera passes with exact precision. He couldn't be sure of getting a match-up between the model footage and the matte footage, except by doing the mattes by hand, one frame at a time.'

Even Perisic concedes the point. 'Getting precision duplicate passes is tricky enough today, with state-of-the-art computerized motion control systems. On *2001* we had enough trouble getting *one* smooth pass, let alone two.'

Trumbull came up with the idea of hand-painting the matte masks, but if they could have done it another way, they would have.

The window action was another challenge. *Discovery*'s control deck was photographed full-scale, from the appropriate angle, with Bowman or Dullea seated at the controls. This footage was then projected, in miniature, from inside the 6-foot diameter command module sphere, onto the back of semi-translucent screens in the window areas. This was the kind of set-up where Veevers excelled. 'When Wally built a rig to suspend a model, or whatever, he did it properly. You knew it would withstand an earthquake. If the footage came out wobbly, you knew it was the camera and not Wally's gear,' says Johnson.

Unfortunately, the exposure required to get a good image of the window action onto the final film was different from that demanded by the model photography as a whole. This meant that the model's movements had to be photographed at least twice onto the same piece of film: first just the model, with the window areas blacked out, and then just the window areas, with the rest of the model draped in black velvet and the camera exposure settings readjusted.

In the spacecraft scenes *prior* to the Jupiter mission, a less complex technique for window action is clearly evident. The *Aries* pasenger shuttle in flight and the moon bus on its way to the Tycho excavation site derive from stills photographs of the models, shot by Keith Hamshere, made into large-format prints, then cut out and pasted onto glass sheets. Using the familiar precision of a flat artwork animation stand, it wasn't hard for Kubrick's Disney-trained animators to combine the window action with the spacecraft images and the star backgrounds. Look carefully at these scenes: the live window action is convincing, while the surrounding space vehicles appear very much like the products of two-dimensional animation. The giveaway is that the perspective of the models never changes. At the time, the effect was still superior to any space sequences that audiences had seen before.

In the final print of *2001*, it's fascinating to see, within a few moments, the range of the effects, from relatively simple to agonizingly complex. The

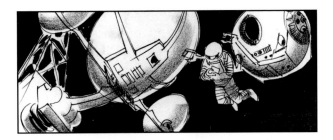

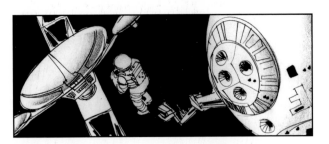

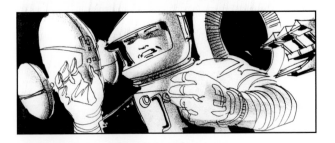

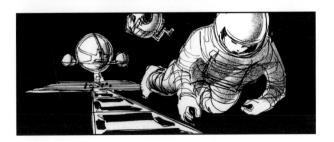

**Getting it down on paper:**
*Storyboards (above) were easy to rough out, but harder to turn into screen images. These panels show a spacewalk sequence. To shoot scenes like these, a live stuntman in a spacesuit had to be combined on film with the 54-foot 'Discovery', a 13-inch pod and a star field.*

**Easily drawn, harder to film:**
*Artists Roy Carnon and Richard McKenna made colour sketches to show what the space scenes in the film might look like. When this space station idea emerged in 1965 (based on a Harry Lange drawing), no one yet knew how it might be rendered on film.*

orbiting satellites and our first view of the *Orion* winged space shuttle are stills photographs, animated in early 1966 while the effects team was still getting into its stride. But a few moments later the rotating space station, shot in late 1966, moves smoothly across the screen; its perspective changes constantly, and the interaction of background stars with the fine tracery of girders in the station's uncompleted section reveals camera motion control and matte work of extraordinary precision. Then, as the *Aries* shuttle carries Heywood Floyd to the moon, the shuttle is another stills photograph cut out and animated.

Proof, if any were needed, that the order in which a film is created bears little resemblance to the sequence in which it is finally presented on screen.

One test reel of effects shots particularly worried Kubrick when he saw it. The space station, rotating on its axis in a delicate ballet, suddenly lurched from one side of the screen to another. 'What the hell was that?' he gasped. Had the massive worm gearings rebelled against their load and snapped? Had the film advance in the camera gate slewed out of alignment? Just for once, the great Kubrick *wasn't* able to think the problem through.

Then someone took a closer look at the log sheets for that effect. It had been shot on a particular weekend where July and August 1966 collided, and Kubrick now remembered that many of his staffers had been unwilling to work that day unless they could wheel a television into the shooting studio to watch football from time to time. It turned out that, as England and

Germany went head to head in the World Cup final, every last technician in the building was glued to that single television. As one, they'd all leaped up to applaud England's winning goal. Meanwhile, on its reinforced shooting stage, the space station had been turning gently for three hours, while the camera snapped doggedly away, at six seconds exposure per frame, for 1,500 frames: enough to generate about a minute's worth of usable footage. And for three frames somewhere about halfway through that 1,500, the studio floor had shaken.

At least the answer to the riddle was there, in the documentation. Vast swathes of paperwork outlined all the details of camera movements, exposure times, film batch colour checks, copy numbers and so on, so that all the sequences could be matched together. Hundreds of shots, exposed but undeveloped, lay in storage inside sealed film cans, while Pederson kept detailed log sheets. As often as not, different shots were photographed many months apart, with the undeveloped film tucked safely into refrigerators between takes. In particular, Trumbull and Pederson single out the wide shots of the lunar astronauts preparing to descend into the Tycho excavation site. After the live action was completed at Shepperton, the film was stored, undeveloped, for nearly two years, until the background lunar hills could be added from separate footage of miniature landscapes, along with stars and a bright blue earth on the horizon.

Kubrick instituted a special command post staffed by expert file handlers. There were all kinds of reference systems: wall charts, rolodexes, pull-out diagrams and card indices, to keep track of the multitude of steps required to complete the various sequences. *American Cinematographer* correspondent Herb Lightman described this large office as 'a huge, throbbing nerve center of a place, with much the same frenetic atmosphere of a Cape Kennedy blockhouse during the final stages of a countdown.' Original first-generation shots of every ship, every star, planet, astronaut or whatever, were carefully logged and stored as original negative film. These were known as the 'masters'. If things went wrong at the positive printing stage, the masters could be brought out and printed again with different exposures and light

intensities. However, a further complication arose every time anything was copied onto fresh film: an intermediate process was used to split the initial shots into three separate black-and-white (monochrome) films, through three separate, tinted filters, one for yellow, one for cyan and one for magenta, the three colours which go to make up a full-colour image. These three reels of monochrome material were referred to as the 'Yellow-Cyan-Magentas' or YCMs'. This film was inherently much sharper than colour stock, and the laborious process helped ensure that the quality of duplicated images was retained. Turning the three monochrome films back into a single colour image required all three layers to be printed down onto fresh colour film, using the relevant colour filtration in the light sources in each case. Thus, many of the masters, stored often for months at a time, were on three sets of film, not one (although star backgrounds only needed one set of film, as they were pure black and white).

The YCM masters also allowed consistent control of the colour balance for all the spacecraft scenes, and there are none of the random

**Forgetting the wheel:**
*For one day at least, the laborious photography of the space station took second place to a sporting victory at the end of July 1966.*

**Trans-Atlantic talent:**
*Con Pederson at his desk,
snapped on high-speed film
by Kubrick in February 1966.*

jumps from warm tones to cold, or from fine grain to rough, that characterized effects sequences in almost every earlier science fiction film. Not surprisingly, the effects department tried to keep multiple copying to a minimum.

For all the spectacular quality of the spaceship shots, the *2001* team did not rely on many radically *new* procedures. Matting, double-exposing and various other techniques have been used for trick photography since the beginning of cinema. Indeed, Kubrick was determined to use the most traditional methods, so that everything could be kept as simple and as controllable as possible—under the circumstances. And since the early movie pioneers never had practical access to complex duplicating processes, they tended to try and get their effects in-camera whenever possible, which was something Kubrick wanted to emulate in order to maintain the sharpness and fine grain of his images. Even the YCM process was related to the earliest methods of producing colour movies, widely in use before Eastman-Kodak introduced straightforward full-colour film in 1951. For instance, *Gone with the Wind* (1939) was shot with a Technicolor camera that split the incoming light three ways, through separate colour filters, onto three reels of black and white film. It was characteristic of Kubrick to take such an interest in essentially old-fashioned techniques. Where some directors would have

seen unnecessary work and expense, he saw instead a number of means to maintain image quality. He was happy to draw inspiration from the brilliant back-yard magic of George Méliès and his *Le Voyage dans la Lune* (1902).

However, one sequence in particular demonstrated an optical procedure that had not been attempted before: the 'Stargate' corridor of light at the film's climax. At the time, this was probably the most spectacular sequence ever created, and as far as the technique was concerned, it was completely innovative.

Arguably the most talked-about effect in the whole movie, the Stargate may well have contributed to the films appeal for the young audiences of 1968. It was a common practice to sidle closer up to the screen just before Dave Bowman started out on his trip, to light up something illegal, and then 'tune in and turn on' while the giant Cinerama screen threw its kaleidoscope of colours at an appreciatively stoned front row.

The drug culture may not quite have been the audience that Clarke and Kubrick were aiming at—they have both outlined their polite but persistent disavowal of drugs—but MGM latched on and marketed the second run of the movie as 'The Ultimate Trip', with unconscious irony hijacking a quote from the *Christian Science Monitor*'s film review.

The Stargate's gyrating tunnel of light was Douglas Trumbull's particular achievement. Kubrick said he wanted the camera to 'go through something', though just what, or how, he didn't specify. He trusted Trumbull to present a range of alternatives, to be rejected, honed down and finally worked into something suitable. This was Kubrick's standard operating procedure with his production staff. It was no good coming to him with a completed concept and thinking, that's that. He would invariably demand alterations, additions or sometimes complete revisions. His attitude was that people never knew what they were capable of achieving if they didn't keep trying, and *he* didn't know precisely what he wanted until he saw it. Trumbull had no particular problems with Kubrick's incessant demands for adaptation (with the possible exception of that scare about going to Saturn instead of Jupiter). For the 'going through something' sequence, he turned his attention to the work of John Whitney, who had been experimenting with long-duration exposures for scientific applications.

Camera buffs will know that there is a marked difference between images that are blurred by motion, and images that are merely out of focus. Some of our best sports photographers rely on deliberately streaking their cyclists, racing cars, horses or whatever, as they swish past the lenses of their Nikons. The images they deliver are perfectly in focus, but the speed and power of their subjects is implied by a certain degree of blur. Though pictures in newspapers and magazines do not move, we have all become accustomed to 'seeing' movement in the blur. John Whitney had applied this technique to certain engineering problems, so that complex events happening over time could be analysed on a single frame of film. He had also explored its artistic possibilities in a series of influential abstract films.

Log sheets show that Trumbull and Perisic began experimenting with single 65mm frames, shot on a vertical animation stand, in January 1967. They shifted the camera left to right and rotated it clockwise and anti-clockwise, with the shutter jammed in its open position. Then they hit on their 'big idea'—moving the camera towards the artwork, or away from it, to create a

*A driven young man: Douglas Trumbull in February 1966.*

blur in depth as well as from side to side. Kubrick was intrigued, and he authorized construction of yet another complex piece of hardware. 'Doug went off and bought a Meccano set,' says Pederson. 'For about £100, we found this huge kit, basically a toy, but you could build just about any kind of mock-up of a mechanical device. He ended up using the same bug-eyed camera that we had used to make the planetarium screen show for the New York World's Fair, which we had brought over with us. He built this huge machine to do time-lapse photography on a very large scale. There was a five-foot long slit with illuminated artwork passing behind it on a conveyor belt. The machine took up a whole studio.'

At one end of the rig, which Trumbull called a 'slit-scan' machine, there was a black-painted metal sheet, about five feet high and ten feet across. A narrow slit was cut into the middle of the sheet. At the other end of the rig was a camera, separated from the metal sheet by the inevitable tracking system of heavy worm gearing (two fifteen-foot monsters, each a couple of hundred pounds in weight, specially flown to London from a machine shop in Detroit). A bank of electrical switches, timers and Selsyn motors controlled the camera's movements along the track. It could move up close to the sheet until it was no more than about four inches away, or it could backtrack to a distance of about twelve feet. The worm gearing ensured that complicated movements could be duplicated time and again. (By now, the motion control concept for accurate multiple passes was delivering on its promise.) The electronic timers were also rigged into the camera controls, so that opening and closing the shutter, advancing the film and so on, could be kept in lock-step with the machine's mechanical movements. The camera also incorporated a device that kept it automatically focused on the slit, no matter how close or how far away it moved along the track, and the shutter was adapted to stay fully open for long stretches.

Behind the slit, yet more mechanisms drove a sheet of artwork, illuminated from behind. For various effects, different kinds of artwork could be stuck down onto this sheet. Typically, geometric Op-Art patterns on paper would first be photographed on a large stills camera in order to yield images as transparencies or, sometimes, as negatives—just so long as a light could be shone through them. With overlays of transparent coloured gels adding to the whole effect, back-lighting then made the artwork glow in a satisfactory way.

Every frame of the Stargate sequence was photographed individually, like a stills picture. The camera would move right up to the slit, then trundle back, allowing the slit to dwindle into the distance until there was nothing much more in shot than a narrow line. And all the time, the camera shutter would remain open with just a single frame of film in place behind it. This produced a satisfying streak on film, giving the illusion of depth. Meanwhile, the illuminated artwork shifted a few inches behind the slit, thereby distorting the image from side to side as

well. At the end of the pass, the shutter would close and the next frame of film would be wound into position.

In the same way that a cartoon animator will repeat frames *almost* exactly, while adding a tiny element of movement, the Selsyn devices of the slit-scan machine were adjusted to add carefully controlled variants to each exposed frame, thus building up a sense of rapid motion when an entire reel of finished and processed footage was projected at 24 frames per second on a movie screen.

One fascinating sequence came tantalizingly close to changing the film's Stargate climax by providing an overt hint of an actual alien community for Bowman to pass through on his way to the hotel room. Trumbull says 'I used the slit-scan to shoot a sequenced array of little light

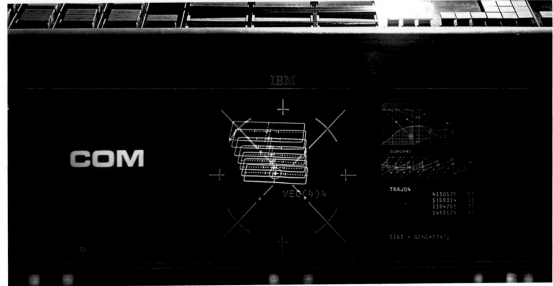

**Screens within screens:** Bruce Logan spent many months preparing 16mm animated sequences for projection into the cockpits. A wide view of the 'Discovery' control deck (above) shows four screens active. The close-up shot (right) shows the 'Orion' docking display.

bulbs, instead of artwork, for what we called the "City of Light". There was some jiggle to the footage and Stanley rejected it, but towards the end of production, he realized there were some good ideas going on here. But we were out of time. As far as I know, a single frame, re-produced in Jerome Agel's book [*The Making of Kubrick's 2001*, 1970] is all that remains of it.'

Trumbull did have time to adapt the slit-scan technique to create a planet. His 'Jupiter Machine' projected artwork of Jupiter's swirling bands of cloud towards a rotating disc. The front and rear faces of the disc were covered in black paint, but the reflective whitened edge caught in the light from the projector. As the disc rotated slowly through 180 degrees, the edge scanned its way across the entire pro-jected image. The camera recorded the edge's blur as it swept through its arc and the result was an amazingly spherical-looking Jupiter. In fact it was too spherical. Pederson says, 'I looked at Jupiter recently through a telescope, and I saw three or four of its orbiting moons. It really brought back memories. Jupiter bulges at the Equator because of its own rotation, and that's evident even through a telescope. When Doug was running the "Jupiter Machine", I fretted about this but Stanley, uncharacter-istically, ignored it.'

Harry Lange remembers that planets in general were a challenge. 'We had so few real NASA images to go on. In particular, the Earth as seen from space worried us a great deal. I thought the Earth in *2001*, which was a very fine piece of artwork by the way, should have been a little more blue, but Stanley had all this scientific data about its exact albedo, its brightness rela-tive to the absolute standard of the sun's brightness. All the boffins said that Earth would be very bright when seen from the Moon. We went with that. How could we have known how *deep* blue the Earth would really seem from the viewpoint of an Apollo moonwalker in 1969, a year after our movie was finished?'

A great deal of the time Stanley and his team relied on brilliant guesswork. There were no established rules for the effects pioneered on *2001*. Exposure meters were useless, and everything had to be tested by trial and error. Stargates, planets, drifting spaceships, tumbling astronauts: all these displays of cinematic wizardry were the result of countless reshoots: re-do's or re-*don'ts* as Kubrick called them, meaning that duff shots were good examples of what *not* to do in later attempts. More than 200 shots in the film involved special effects work, each one requiring about ten separate steps to complete: 2,000 steps in all. Taking into con-sideration the times when things had to be done again or tinkered with in some way, the number of individual steps logged by Kubrick's command post came to something like sixteen thousand by the end of production. As Doug Trumbull remarked after it was all over, 'It was a case of do it right, then do it better, then do it all over again.'

Even today, with so many advances in cinema and video technology at our disposal, *2001*'s special effects and tumbling sets still look impressive. Certainly, modern film makers can now achieve equally spectacular images in a fraction of the time, for a fraction of the cost. They can even do better, with powerful com-puters and new digital imaging techniques. But at the end of the day, what counts? Realism, sharp focus, believability: the essential optical considerations for any major piece of cinema. Modern audiences don't have to make any mental allowances for Kubrick's effects. They can still be taken at face value.

The smooth effects mask a certain amount of underlying turmoil. Veevers and Howard were much-admired in the 1960s film industry, and their contributions to *2001* were critical, yet there seems to have been a generational clash between them and the young Americans from Graphic Films. Veevers and Howard 'knew' from long experience how effects were supposed to be done, while the trans-Atlantic kids wanted to test new ideas. Some of the older folk were surprised at the speed with which Trumbull, in particular, seemed ready to turn his hand to any new task going.

Veevers was working on the assumption that the individual spacecraft shots should be created according to a preconceived story-board, a rough sketch showing the positions of the various elements, derived from the narrative within the script. Masters, Pederson and

Trumbull were all adept at storyboarding and Kubrick found the boards useful up to a point. But he wanted a wide range of spacecraft angles, speeds and compositions, just as he would expect a range of live-action shots of actors. He didn't want to be constrained in the editing process by a predetermined lack of choice. Veevers didn't always understand this.

'Wally was rather like a "Mr Bumble", quite large, very rotund, softly spoken', says Hamshere. 'His background was engineering, but he was also extremely artistic. He was a precise man, very creative, but also sensitive. He sometimes found it hard to put into words what he was trying to achieve. He and Stanley respected each other one hundred per cent, but of all the people on the film, I think there was probably more friction between him and Stanley than anyone else.'

Veevers also had an irascible temper at times. It didn't help that Kubrick had a knack for encouraging insurrection among the younger technicians. Brian Johnson remembers helping Veevers to set up the little 16mm film projectors that beamed HAL9000's computer displays onto the centrifuge control panels. 'Wally had this elaborate system with different focal-length lenses on different projectors because we couldn't stack them as close to each other as the HAL read-outs actually appear in the film. Anyway, I said, "Why don't we bolt pairs of projectors base to base, to keep them arranged as tightly as possible? That way, their lenses will be close together, and we can use the same length of lens on all the machines." Wally said you couldn't operate projectors upside-down. They all had to be upright, and that was that. But later, I thought, "Wait a minute! The rotation of the centrifuge will spin them upside-down at some point anyway, so what difference does it make?" So I took that idea to Stanley, and he went with my idea. Wally didn't speak to me for days.' (Veevers wasn't wrong, though. Upside-down, the bulbs lasted about three minutes apiece, until adaptations were made to the 16mm projectors.)

Trumbull confesses that 'one of the major factors in the delay and climbing budget was that a lot of things were being made up as we went along. Things kept changing to accommodate new ideas.' This echoes Fred Ordway's frustrated diary entry about the Art Department's struggles with the spacecraft designs. Others shared this disquiet, and there were resignations. Victor Lyndon told the *Daily Express* in 1968 'I've never known a film where there were so many sackings.' Lyndon generally had to perform this function himself, maybe a couple of dozen times in all, because Kubrick found the task 'too distressing'. In the end, Lyndon reached his own limit. Having started out on *2001* with great enthusiasm, he ended up chasing quality control on the processing of the YCM separations. It was repetitive, immensely tedious work, and he longed for it to be over.

It's not that people were genuinely dissatisfied. Making *2001* was such a tremendous adventure, it was a great career break for the kids, there were all these toys to play with, and Stanley was such a generous and funny and wonderful guy, and so on and so forth. But after being imprisoned so long at Borehamwood slaving on the mechanical and optical effects, Kubrick's technicians were exhausted, and this led to frayed nerves all round. 'Everything had to be absolutely, spotlessly perfect', says Trumbull. 'There wasn't a fleck of dust on any of the artwork, there were never any technical flaws, or jiggles to the movement, or bad lighting. And we had to shoot over and over until everything was perfect in all respects. It was gruelling. After two and a half years of non-stop work, the crew was beginning to show the strain. Towards the end of the film, in the last few months, there was a lot of anxiety and antagonism. People were saying they were tired of it—that it had gone on too long, that it was too agonizing, too difficult.'

Even Pederson, among the most enthusiastic and unstinting of Kubrick's collaborators, was ready to call it a day. 'I was worn out. At the beginning of '68 I went back to California and took a couple of years off from the movie business. I got to know the High Sierras like the back of my hand.'

Frustrations aside, most of the huge *2001* production team had a pretty good time. As Johnson recalls, 'We all knew we were working on something truly significant, something that would make all the strains worthwhile.' Keith Hamshere sums up the prevailing mood:

'Stanley could drive you absolutely nuts, but when you saw the completed footage you just thought, "Wow! That's fantastic!" It was worth all the pain and heartache.'

However, some additional minor tensions emerged *after* the film's release. At the 1969 Oscar ceremonies, Kubrick collected the statuette for Best Visual Effects on behalf of all the supervisors. According to the Oscar rules then in place, there were too many special effect

that he doesn't feel remotely aggrieved about the nominations. Unfortunately, Trumbull lost contact with Kubrick during the 1970s after a sad and rather ironic misunderstanding. 'I never claimed to be the only guy who worked on *2001*, but the press always simplifies things. "Doug Trumbull, who did the effects for *2001*". Well, Stanley would read these articles and he'd write, or phone me up, and he'd say, "What are you doing, going round claiming to be the only

**Cosmic unease:**
*Kubrick and his effects team tried to capture the inhuman loneliness and terror of deep space. In particular, Poole's lifeless body appears to drift in a silent and infinite void.*

credits to be taken into account. Yet there had been no problem nominating Tony Masters, Harry Lange and Ernie Archer individually for their production design. Had they won, each could have emerged from the awards ceremony clutching his own Oscar. Veevers, Howard, Trumbull and Pederson deserved awards, and Kubrick certainly should have walked away with the Oscar for Best Picture. One cannot avoid the feeling that a single Oscar to Kubrick for Best Visual Effects was an inadequate accolade.

'That's been a touchy issue,' Trumbull admits. 'I don't think it was an appropriate credit for him to have taken. The effects weren't de-signed by Kubrick, they were *directed* by him. I think it was one of the rare times in movie history when a director was so integrally involved in the effects, but it was a collaborative process involving a lot of people.'

Pederson says much the same, although with a different emphasis. 'Stanley directed *all* the effects on the film. There should never be any question about that.' From his tone, it is clear

guy who did the special effects?" And I'd have to tell him, over and over, that I'd never said that. But afterwards, we never really spoke.'

Back in the spring of 1968 it looked, for a while, as if there wasn't much point in arguing about the credits anyway. Pederson remembers *2001*'s difficult first reception: 'A lot of what looks like science fiction these days is really car chases. It's the accepted concept of action and adventure. The phrase "art film" is like a dirty word in Hollywood, because nobody would go and see one if they thought of it that way, but that's what we had just made, on a huge scale. In marketing terms, I think it was an accident that *2001* was successful. No one quite knew what they were looking at, and they really didn't know how to view it.'

'I was very disappointed to hear that the movie wasn't going well', says Trumbull. 'They were about thirty days into the release and maybe only a few days away from abandoning it altogether because it wasn't doing business. It was playing to empty theatres. But then some

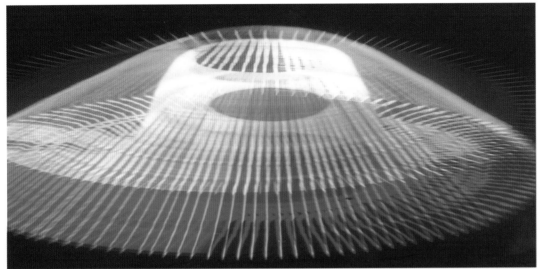

*Sliding towards success:*
*Trumbull and Zoran Perisic*
*experimented with an ordinary*
*animation stand, shifting a*
*camera with its shutter open*
*to create interesting blur effects*
*from illuminated artwork. This*
*is one of the frames that*
*persuaded Kubrick to fund*
*the slit-scan machine.*

kind of word of mouth started picking up, and the theatre managers all said, "Well, let's give it a few more days and see what happens." And after that, it picked up and found its audience. But it was a close call.'

Another aspect of the movie's first release took the *2001* team by suprise—the Cinerama projection system. The Cinerama logo on *2001*'s publicity posters is based on the format's original concept: three projectors in a movie theatre throwing images onto three screens, side by side, to generate a very wide overall picture. Original photography required a trio of cameras in parallel, and the whole thing was a gimmick designed to compete with the late 1950s growth of domestic television viewing at the expense of trips to the cinema. By the mid-1960s, when *2001* was filmed, Cinerama had been adapted along more straightforward lines. Only one reel of film was required, and a special lens in the theatre projector threw a single super-wide image onto a giant screen that curved to such an extent it all but enveloped the audience.

Quite apart from his habitual fascination with new optical systems, Kubrick agreed to make *2001* in Cinerama after the success of an earlier film, *How The West Was Won*, triggered MGM's interest in the new, simplified format. (His jokey nickname for *2001* at one point was *How The Solar System Was Won*, in honour of the wide-screen cowboys he was supposed to supplant

at the box office.) *2001* was photographed on a 65mm noise-proofed Super Panavision camera for sound synchronization, or a 65mm Mitchell camera for scenes and effects not requiring lip-synchronized dialogue. The final Cinerama prints, with the completed dialogue and music tracks running down the side, were released on 70mm film, but the production's daily 'rushes' were reduced onto 35mm and projected onto a normal flat screen. It would have been far too expensive to make Cinerama prints merely for rushes. As Trumbull recalls, 'We never had a chance during production to see a proper projection. In a sense, you could say that we didn't really have the curved screen in mind while we made the movie. In some of the Cinerama theatres there was a serious problem because the projection booths were mounted up too high and you had a horrible sort of curved, warping effect. The titles, credits and so on would come out badly distorted.'

Fortunately, the perspectives of the film's ultra-wide-angle photography were so extreme already that the distortion couldn't do much damage. And for all the fuss generated about Cinerama over the years, it's worth noting that many people who saw *2001* thirty years ago didn't watch it in the super-wide format, but on more conventional screens showing 35mm prints. Only the largest cities around the world could afford theatres large enough to accommodate Cinerama, with its specially adapted 70mm projector and huge screen.

# 2001: filming the future

The very last images of the film are perhaps the most powerful and startling of all—that moment when Dave Bowman is reborn as a glowing 'Starchild'. The internal luminescence of this bright creature was generated by powerful back-lighting. When the baby turns its head towards the audience for a final awe-inspiring gaze, we register that as a brief, heart-stopping few moments, ten seconds or so, which took eight hours to film. The light shining into the back of the resin sculpture gradually made the whole thing glow, but only after very long exposures for each frame of film. The child's enveloping aura was a superimposed piece of artwork, double-exposed onto the footage later.

Harry Lange's wife Daisy loves to tell a story about the Starchild during photography. The back-lighting was intense, and the sculpture rotated very slowly on a motorized podium. A young camera operator was equipped with a can of insect repellent (at Kubrick's insistence, to keep flies from settling on the baby) and left to get on with the job, hour after hour. Click. Click. Click. Three frames a second, so that the backlighting could really burn in and make the baby glow. 'Unknown to the cameraman, the Starchild's glass eyes were stuck into its head with candle wax, or some such, and it started to melt under the lights. It looked like the baby was crying real tears. And when this poor young man saw that, he ran out of the studio, screaming at the top of his lungs. Come to think of it, I'm sure he was a devout Catholic.'

The Starchild was sculpted by a young, talented and vivacious artist, Liz Moore, who has never been properly credited. She was a well-loved member of the *2001* crew. Kubrick was sufficiently impressed to hire her for his next film. She sculpted the shocking and rather less edifying 'nude' furniture for *A Clockwork Orange* (for which she did receive a screen credit). A few years later she was killed in a car crash while working on Richard Attenborough's *A Bridge Too Far* (1977). Her principal legacy in the film business is 20 seconds of footage at the end of *2001*. But those 20 seconds remain one of the most memorable images in all of cinema.

Of course the cast of characters from the production has thinned out over the three decades since *2001* was made. Tony Masters,

Wally Veevers, Geoffrey Unsworth, John Alcott, Derek Cracknell, Victor Lyndon, along with actors Leonard Rossiter and William Sylvester, have died in recent years. Some of these names may be in danger of fading from memory, but their professional and creative contributions to the art of cinema will linger in our imaginations for a long while yet.

'I can't believe how long ago it all was,' says Hamshere. 'The film looks so fresh, as if we'd only made it yesterday. But a short while ago I was in California, and someone came up to me and said, "You knew my grandfather, Tommy Howard!" I've never felt so old in all my life.'

***Toying with an idea:***
*Kubrick in his office, holding a plastic baby doll which he used to explore shooting options for the Starchild.*

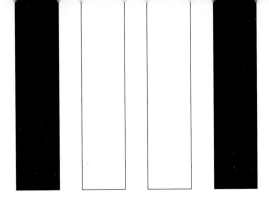

# 6: out of africa

IF DOUG TRUMBULL was the 'driven young man' of the special effects department, he more than found his match in Andrew Birkin, one of Kubrick's several young assistants. Brother to actress Jane Birkin, he was a perpetual tearaway and hanger-on at the fringes of the louche 1960s European movie world, and had travelled widely by the time he was nineteen. He seemed ill-adjusted for any steady job of work, getting by on his charm and casual social connections in the movie business. And then he entered the world of *2001: A Space Odyssey*.

At first, it didn't seem that much of a life-changing break. 'A friend of mine got me a job as runner and teaboy for the princely sum of $15 per week. For about six weeks, I operated a photostat machine, and that was about it. I was going mad with boredom and I was ready to quit. I hadn't even met the great Kubrick. All I'd done so far was wind the clock in his office when he wasn't there.'

At the close of each day's shooting, he wandered dreamily around *2001*'s huge spacecraft sets. He wasn't allowed near them during working hours, because he had few useful functions on set apart from delivering tea and call sheets. Worse still, he didn't have a union card. He was fascinated by what he saw, but his prospects in the movie business were not improved when he accidentally sealed himself into a space pod during one of his illegal visits.

In February 1966 he was delivering yet more tea to one of the shooting stages where, for some reason that wasn't immediately apparent to him, a new set had just been constructed, with a giant artwork of rocks and desert for a background. Production designer Ernie Archer, art director John Hoesli, and construction manager Cliff Brandon had spent thousands of pounds building the set, but Kubrick, on hand for a first inspection, was edgy. 'Forget it. This won't work. There must be a location somewhere that we could use instead of this? Does anyone know, are there any desert-type terrains in England?'

His disconsolate designers shrugged their shoulders. 'To this day I don't know why I did it,' Birkin says, 'But I shouted, "Yes! There *is* somewhere we can go." And Stanley asked "Where?" And I said I could find the information at home.'

As soon as he could get away, Birkin caught a train to an industrial site outside Liverpool, which, by chance, he'd seen illustrated in an old school geography textbook. With a borrowed Polaroid camera, he snapped the site—a mixture of shallow scrub and dunes of sand, spoiled only by an enormous gasworks in the background—then glued his shots to a board and wrote up some notes. Taking the pre-dawn 'milk train' back to London next morning, he left his amateurish compilation on Kubrick's desk. Suddenly his little expedition didn't seem like

**Our unruly ancestors:**
*Two bands of apemen fight for possession of a muddy waterhole in the opening scenes of the film.*

such a good idea. By now, he had a pretty clear sense of what his director needed. On reflection, maybe that patch of Liverpudlian waste ground wasn't much like a prehistoric desert after all. Birkin crept out of Kubrick's office feeling faintly foolish. Not expecting to deserve his costs, he nevertheless delivered receipts for $10 in rail tickets and bed-and-breakfast accommodation to the *2001* accounts department.

But that night, Victor Lyndon called him at home. 'I don't know what you've been up to, but Stanley says we should give you a union card and triple your salary.' Reporting for work next morning, he was summoned into the privileged world of the art department, where Kubrick was playing a little game with his designers, Tony Masters, Ernie Archer and Harry Lange. 'I don't know, guys. It's taken you five months and ten thousand dollars to come up

with nothing. Then the teaboy gives me an answer in one day, for ten dollars and change.'

Kubrick knew he was being mischievous. Birkin's location *was* useless. Nevertheless, after he'd had his fun with his designers, he took the young man aside. 'Do you know how to use a real camera?'

'Yes.'

'Do you know about different film stocks? Emulsions? Processing?'

'Um—no, but I'd love to learn.'

'Okay, I'll send you over to the Technicolor lab for a couple of days. They'll teach you.'

That was it. From now on, as long as he didn't screw up, Birkin was a *bona fide* Kubrick protégé. The crew immediately began to take him more seriously, and he learned from them at a ferocious pace, with a hunger that suprised him as much as any of his colleagues. With his union card approved, and empowered by the heady new rank of 'Third Assistant Director', he began the challenging task of helping to log 2001's special effects. Perhaps for the first time in his life 'I wanted to accept responsibility for something that was much bigger than myself.'

Another duty was to carry on scouting various potential locations within Britain that might suit 2001's requirements. He travelled to Bangor in North Wales, armed with fifty packs of Polaroid film, looking for that elusive desert, and also visited several of Britain's most imposing country houses.

For the moonbase scenes, Kubrick was interested in showing the family life of lunar colonists, and he wondered how 21st century space planners would create pleasant living and communal areas, as well as the inevitable control rooms and docking bays. He decided that a few luxuries might be transported to the Moon to make life for its underground inhabitants more palatable. Among the delights on offer would be a garden with real grass, ducks and geese, and an ornamental stone pond. On September 27, 1966 actor William Sylvester, a dozen 'extras' and seven children (including a brace of Kubrick daughters) arranged themselves in front of Luton Hoo country house in Bedfordshire, which had a pond that met with Kubrick's approval. At the top of the steps leading up to the house, riggers built a section of the moonbase interior, including a lift doorway and some wall panels. Wally Veevers was on hand to ensure that the footage of the pond, with the lift doorway in the background, would eventually 'marry up' by a matte process with the larger moonbase interiors at Borehamwood.

In the novel of 2001, Dave Bowman's hotel room, with its somewhat vulgarly baroque trappings of elegance, is a snapshot of supposedly luxurious living derived from alien observations of Earth's television shows. Luton Hoo's ornamental pond, transported to the Moon via special effects, was supposed to presage the hotel room's decor, but as Kubrick and Clarke slashed at their script, removing any literal explanations for the film's climax, the Luton Hoo scenes were dropped. Bangor also fell by the wayside. However, Birkin's location scouting for 2001 had only just begun.

In late 1966 he was chatting to Bryan Loftus, one of the senior effects technicians. Loftus had been tinkering with the YCM separations, printing them in the wrong order, or with the filters deliberately misaligned, to create distorted colours in the positive prints. These experiments didn't have much to do with the work in hand, but Birkin persuaded him to take the test prints to Kubrick, who liked what he saw. By the end of November 1966, Birkin was shooting aerial footage of the Outer Hebrides landscape for what became known as the 'Purple Heart' sequence during Dave Bowman's mindwarping trip to the hotel room. 'Suddenly I had a budget for three days in a helicopter, a camera operator to boss about, and all this responsibility. For two days the weather was terrible and we couldn't fly. On the third day I told the pilot "fly anyway." I was determined to get the shots. Everyone kept asking me, "Andrew, do you have kids?" And I said, no, I didn't. And they said, "Well, why are you risking your neck in a helicopter in rotten weather just for a film?" But I was determined to get my job done.'

He brought his shots home, and the effects department applied Loftus's deliberate YCM misadjustments to the footage, creating the effect of an eerie alien landscape.

The young Birkin's next location trip was even more ambitious.

The Dawn of Man prologue to 2001 is set four million years ago, in an arid landscape deep in the heart of a continent that would one day be called Africa. Chief cinematographer Geoffrey Unsworth had completed his work on the production by the time these sequences were ready for filming. He had shot solidly from Christmas 1965 up until July 1966, and was now required for another production, The Great Train Robbery. His assistant, John Alcott, remained to oversee the Dawn of Man photography. (This was the start of a long working relationship between Alcott and Kubrick.)

From February 1967 till the end of May, Birkin and production designer Ernie Archer were despatched on 'safari' with Paris-based Life photographer Pierre Boulat, to bring back large format transparency photographs of sky and landscape from specially selected areas of the Namibian desert in south-west Africa, which Kubrick now intended to use as a new and more convincing backdrop for the *Dawn of Man* settings at Borehamwood.

As if to highlight the difficulties of location shooting that Kubrick was habitually so keen to avoid, Boulat broke his legs when his truck ran head-on into another vehicle, deep in the heart of the desert. The two vehicles involved were the only motorized transport for many miles around. 'If anything can go wrong, it will', was a Kubrick motto. 'Don't save the day. Anticipate it.' Birkin saved and anticipated as best he could, far from home. He had been assigned total responsibility for transportation, equipment, the camping gear and the budget—practically everything on the shoot except taking the actual photographs. The sheets of film had to be kept cool, and zealous customs authorities at every stage of the air freight route between London and Africa had to be prevented, somehow, from opening the film boxes and fogging the contents. His crew had to sleep rough most of the time, the food was poor, funds weren't getting through from London on time, because MGM had no formal relationship with the local banks, and to cap it all, he had lost his principal stills photographer plus half his vehicles. Now he *really* had to start thinking on his feet.

John Cowan, a London-based photographer (whose fashionable studio was used for Antonioni's film *Blow-Up*) arrived a few days later to replace Boulat. His relationship with Birkin and Archer wasn't a success. Kubrick and Lyndon politely fired him by airmail ('we understand that other urgent commitments prevent you from working with us further') and despatched Keith Hamshere to replace him. At last, things started going Birkin's way. A comprehensive range of ten-by-eight-inch transparencies was returned to Kubrick in England, to his eventual satisfaction. Archer, Birkin and Hamshere flew back to London at the end of May, exhausted but sure that they'd done the job. (Cable to Victor Lyndon: HAVE ARRIVED SAFELY JOHANNESBURG STOP TWO HOURS LATE FOR CONNECT FLIGHT STOP FULL BODY SEARCH AT AIRPORT STOP.)

For Birkin, this African adventure was the beginning of a sucessful career in films, both as director and scriptwriter. 'That was Stanley's knack—to give you a break if you were halfway interested in accepting the challenge, or if you showed any kind of willingness or curiosity to participate in what he was doing. After *2001*, I never looked back, and I owe the start of my real career to him.'

Once Kubrick had made his selection from the Namibian shots, he set about the task of transforming a little-used photographic technique into one of the largest and most extraordinary optical effects ever conceived. Audiences never knew at the time that the vast landscapes, distant horizons and blazing skies of *2001*'s opening scenes were realized deep within the confines of a drizzle-soaked London suburb in autumn. In the process of 'front projection' pioneered for *2001*, the apeman actors were photographed in front of a huge screen, 40 feet high and 100 feet wide, consisting of millions of microscopic glass beads, which absorbed light, bent it, and then hurled it back out again along exactly the same path as it first arrived, with negligible loss of brightness. Kubrick's researchers had come across a suitable new material originally patented by the 3M company for use on reflective roadsigns. To begin with, several rolls were pasted onto the screen in 100-foot lengths, but slight differences in manufacturing tolerances between one batch of material and another produced an uneven, stripy effect. Kubrick ordered the whole lot torn down, whereupon the hundreds of square yards of material were cut up into small jagged shapes, then glued back onto the screen as an intermingled patchwork to achieve a more consistent blend.

A transparency of an appropriate backdrop was projected onto this glassy surface, just as with a home slide projector—except that *2001*'s front-projection machine bore the same relation to a domestic system as a flamethrower does to a match. Kubrick and Tom Howard designed a projector to take the high-definition ten-by-eight-inch Ektachrome transparencies returned from Namibia by Archer and Hamshere. Imagine the comparison between such a system and the 35mm carousel projectors we are all familiar with. Only by beaming transparencies more or less the size of the page you are now reading could Kubrick hope to avoid grain and blur.

Illumination was derived from a powerful arc-lamp similar to the kind of bulb found in an anti-aircraft searchlight. A major worry was that the bulb threw out an intense blast of heat as well as light. Cooling systems protected the projector's lenses from cracking in the heat. Reserve copies of favoured transparencies had to be on stand-by before they could be risked in the projector itself, in case their emulsion layers melted or their glass mountings cracked. Once the machine was powered up, the slightest change in ambient temperature could create havoc. On one occasion the door to the shooting studio was opened by mistake, and a blast of cool autumnal air swept past the super-hot machinery. The lenses immediately shattered—just as an expensive wine glass washed in warm water will splinter if it is accidentally rinsed under the cold tap.

Just as fragile was a slanted mirror in front of the Panavision camera lens, which bounced the projector beam so that it fired in exactly the same direction as the camera was pointing; because the mirror was only half-silvered, the camera could still see through it. From the camera's point of view, the *Dawn of Man* apemen perfectly masked their own shadows on the reflective screen—and *around* the apes, the Namibian desert scenery bouncing back from the screen was clearly visible to the camera. The apemen's dark costumes did not reflect any of this image, even when they were standing close to the projector. As a final touch, the foreground lighting on the set was arranged with great care to match the original sun angle and daylight conditions in the projected background.

For the apeman actors on set, the whole business was distinctly eerie. Unless they happened to look exactly along the axis that the camera was pointing, they couldn't see anything of the front-projected image behind them. The screen just looked like a blank white wall.

The ever-patient Ernie Archer designed and built the foreground sets of rocks, pools and caves on a 90-foot diameter rotating platform, so that widely differing pieces of scenery could be brought in front of the giant screen without moving the front projection rig or the reflective

screen between set-ups. (Another notable scene in *2001*, depicting astronauts walking on the lunar surface with their base in the background, was also achieved with front projection.)

While Stuart Freeborn and his son Graham developed the apeman costumes under conditions of heightened security, Kubrick and Howard worked on building the projector. Meanwhile, IBM granted Kubrick access to an irresistible new toy, a giant computer used for calculating payrolls and other data for big businesses. He fed the *Dawn of Man* budgets, materials requirements, staffing levels and so forth into the machine, and it calculated that, given the current rate of working and the prevailing man-hours per task, everything could be completed in four years. How everybody laughed. How everybody cried.

Kubrick also had trouble finding the right performers. Journalist Victor Davis took up the story in the *Daily Express*, April 18, 1968:

*Research suggested that the creatures should be more man than ape—a nude with a sparse covering of hair. The hard-pressed make-up department presented 75 examples for Kubrick's inspection. He blanched. The cavorting actors presented a fair facsimile of a Mau-Mau orgy in progress. Kubrick solved the nudity problem by putting the actors into monkey suits. But he also decided that the performers should not be more than five feet tall, and should have long upper lips to carry the simian make-up. He mused, 'The Irish have long upper lips. Get me 50 five-foot Irish actors with long upper lips.' The Dublin agencies were combed, but most of the mini-apemen were found nearer home. The first was diminutive Ronnie Corbett, the TV comedian, then a relatively unknown entertainer.*

Corbett was interviewed by Kubrick. 'I want you for a major role in my film. You will be the first man. It's—er—a most tender and moving role.' The comedian submitted to a series of tests in which he donned mock-up costumes 'like hairy combinations.' The production secretaries screamed at the sight of him, and he was released from any further obligations.

Eventually, it was Daniel Richter who played 'the first man' and threw the bone that propelled us into the future (after murdering his rival at the waterhole, played by Richard Wood). A young mime actor from Connecticut in thrall to Lee Strasburg's 'method' school of acting, Richter came aboard in early 1967 and immediately transformed the casting of Kubrick's apemen. He had developed a naturalistic mime technique, far removed from the tragi-comical traditions of Marcel Marceau and other practitioners. 'Stanley's right-hand man Victor Lyndon contacted me, and I found out that they'd tried all kinds of costumes, and various stuntmen and dancers, and it hadn't been a success. You couldn't just have dancers making movements up as they went along, and I saw this essentially as an *acting* problem. You had to make the performers think and feel like apemen. Method acting isn't something that you'd associate with Stanley, but when I put these ideas to him, he was immediately impressed.'

Richter began studying everything he could find on anthropology and evolution. 'There was a debate about how much these creatures should look like apes, or men. In 1967, we didn't know anything like as much as we do today about human origins. A lot of it was inspired guesswork.' He agreed with Kubrick (and the IBM budget calculations) that an African location shoot for a troope of apeman actors in heavy costumes was out of the question, on grounds of safety and cost. After being sworn to secrecy, he was briefed on the emerging front-projection scheme, and then installed in his own rehearsal space at Borehamwood, in charge of 20 actors and dancers. 'The dancers were already pretty fit, but the actors needed toughening up. In the end, I just put 'em all through a process like an army boot camp.'

After physical exercises at Borehamwood in the morning, the entire squad would spend afternoons at London Zoo in Regents Park, studying the primate collection. Richter took careful note of every gesture and grimace: 'Guy the Gorilla was my inspiration and mentor, you might say.' He then tutored his band of actors, day after day, until they hardly knew the difference anymore between human and animal ways of behavior. 'It took about three months,

and by the end of it, you could have picked up all these guys and dropped them in the middle of Picadilly Circus, and they would have gone right on functioning—stealing food from passers-by, fighting among themelves. I didn't choreograph them, I *created* an actual tribe, with relationships, a social order, and a pre-human way of thinking. They really bonded. They thought I was a little bit aloof from them, and that was deliberate.'

Fellow apeman Simon Willis confirms this. 'Yes, Dan kept himself to himself, but his approach really worked. Andy Wallace [another ape-actor] and I would get up from the table after a meal, and we constantly found ourselves pushing against the tabletop with our knuckles. It came so naturally to us, it was quite scary. We even had our backs arched like apes without even thinking about it.'

Rehearsals called for arduous squatting and jumping, and only very rarely a fully erect bipedal stance. It was painful and demanding on human muscles that had long since evolved out of those postures. Richter also insisted on constant energy from his troupe. 'It was essential for the audience to believe in the man-apes in the first few minutes. I thought the way to solve the problem was to give them the same kind of restlessness and perpetual movement that you find in real animals when they're awake. Compared to animals, humans walking down the street hardly move at all.'

While Richter taught his peformers to act like animals, Kubrick searched for animals who could perform like actors. Victor Lyndon's pre-production notes required:

*A leopard or lioness to do the following tricks: snarl, leap and, if possible, fight with a 'man-ape'. Grazing animals to mix with our 'man-apes' in the field. 4 warthogs to be trained.*

Arthur Clarke read this, and noted in his diary 'Glad that's not *my* job.' A quartet of tapirs eventually got the grazing contract. Kubrick didn't seem too worried about this strange version of prehistoric Africa, where leopards and lions were supposed to co-exist with creatures from South America.

Terry Duggan, an expert animal trainer, joined Richter's gang and had the distinction of playing the first of *2001*'s eight murder victims. Duggan brought with him a handsome young leopard whose main task was to leap off a promontory and 'kill' him as prey. 'That scene had to be kept very short in the final cut of the movie,' Richter says. 'It wasn't because of any danger from the leopard—he was happy to roll around chewing on Terry all afternoon, just playfighting. He knew he wasn't supposed to chew too hard. Our problem was that Terry had a stocky build, and he didn't look quite right in the costume.'

In Kubrick's 'Notes on Special Effects' delivered as part of his 1969 Academy Award submissions, he said that Duggan and the leopard were entirely alone on stage during the shoot, just in case the leopard went for one of the other actors. Background performers were added later, after the hand-drawn matte technique had been applied to Duggan and his leaping leopard.

The leopard's other job was to sit next to a horse carcass, painted up as a zebra, pretending he had killed it. It turned out that when he stared directly towards the front-projector beam, the retinal layers at the back of his eyes demonstrated the same kind of reflectivity as the glass beads in the 3M screen behind him. Literally, he had 'cat's eyes'. He looked suitably impressive looming in the twilight over his victim with his eyes ablaze. But he wasn't too keen on staying in place, because the horse carcass was

past its prime. Meanwhile, for his apeman companions, the stench of rotting flesh was much closer to home, as Davis recalls only too vividly. 'The meat we were supposedly chewing smelled bad because of the heat in the studio. It was hard not to gag with nausea. Obviously we didn't have to swallow it for real, but traces of fat became stuck in the teeth of your mask, and after a while it absolutely stank.'

These meat-eating scenes were supposedly the result of a new-found prowess with bone cudgels. Moonwatcher's weapon was an allegory of all the technology created by humanity, but no one can recall precisely how that idea was developed. 'Going into those sequences, we never knew where it would fit into the overall movie,' says Richter. 'But I certainly realized that something had caught Stanley's imagination when he started to focus more and more on the bone. We spent a long time shooting many different angles and arm movements and throws. We did a *lot* of throwing. I threw some, Stanley threw some. Everyone had a throw at some point. I knew he needed to move the story four million years into the future, but I didn't know exactly how he was going to do it. I don't even know if *he* knew at that point. I wish he was still around so that I could ask him how his mind was working.'

Davis played a 'mother' ape, clutching a real young chimpanzee. He thinks that this single genuine ape working amidst the gang of human imposters may have inspired the sequence. 'Once, when they were relighting the set, and it was still dressed and ready for a shoot, our baby chimp started playing with a pile of small bones that were on the set. You know how chimps flail their arms sometimes when they're playing? She picked one up and threw it in the air. Mr Kubrick saw that, but you could never tell what might be going through his mind.'

At the 1969 Oscar ceremonies, during which *2001* inexplicably failed to sweep the board, the greatest insult of all was when 20th Century Fox's *Planet of the Apes* won an award for its mass-produced gorilla masks. This was a nasty shock, bearing in mind the effectiveness of Freeborn's apemen. The Academy's decision was a real injustice. After the awards ceremony, Arthur

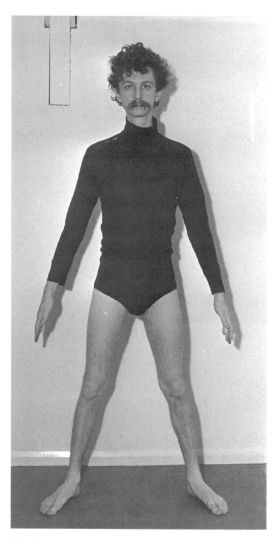

***The man behind the mask:*** *Dan Richter poses before clambering into his apeman costume.*

Clarke went round muttering his dissatisfaction as loudly as he could. 'What did they think we used—*real* apes?'

According to Richter 'There was a lot of paranoia while we were preparing *The Dawn of Man*. We didn't know for sure, but we thought we were being watched by the *Planet of the Apes* people. Parts of our costumes did go missing and Stanley went ballistic. Once a helicopter flew over us while we were in the open, and we all dived for cover.' Davis remembers Kubrick hearing the chopper and running out of his office, shouting to the troupe, 'Hit the deck, you guys! It's 20th Century Fox!'

After the failed 'Mau-Mau orgy' experiments, Freeborn's costumes ended up rather more 'ape' than 'man'. He created masks with tiny

levers that the actors inside could move with their lips and teeth. In response, the masks' artificial lips pulled back to reveal large snarling teeth. The ape-like jaws and snouts extended far beyond any human shape, but the eye sockets fitted exactly around the actors' eyes. Those with brown eyes had the better time of it. Blue eyes required masking with brown contact lenses made from hard glass. As a final flourish, the pelt of the costumes was woven from a convincing mixture of animal and artificial hairs.

Kubrick may have given up his search for Irishmen with long upper lips by the time Richter took charge of the troupe, but with the notable exception of Terry Duggan, the apeman performers consisted almost entirely of short, thin men with long thin arms. They looked just right for 2001's evolutionary theme: more than mere brutes, yet less than fully human.

In June 1967 Birkin's principal involvement with 2001 came to an end. He received a note from Kubrick's office acknowledging 'the way in which you handled an arduous and uncomfortable location in Africa, under, to say the least, very difficult conditions.' Birkin was all of 22 years old.

**The evolutionary chain:**
*Despite the many months that separated filming of the apeman and spaceman scenes, Kubrick never lost sight of his central idea—that even the blandest astronauts are still little more than clever apes in disguise, with ancient survival instincts hard-wired into their brains.*

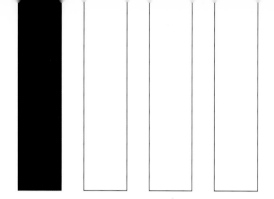

# 7 : walking on the walls

THE MECHANICAL EFFECTS in *2001* were just as complex, and considerably more dangerous for the stuntmen, camera crews and actors enmeshed in them. The difference between optical illusion and real technology became increasingly blurred. *Discovery*'s centrifuge sequences, for instance, were filmed in a huge revolving drum mounted on its edge, as high as a house: nearly forty feet in diameter, and twenty feet wide. It was specially constructed by Vickers Engineering at a cost of over $750,000 (which ate up rather a large chunk of the film's budget). The actual shooting set was somewhat narrower, sandwiched in the middle of the drum like the cream in a sponge cake. The 'sponge' areas were stuffed literally to the brim with lights and electrical equipment, along with two dozen separate film projectors which provided graphics displays for the interior control consoles. All of the fixtures, read-outs, desks and couches had to rotate with the entire set.

The outside of the drum was a complex mountain of scaffolding, metal struts, access platforms and ladders. The whole structure was swaddled in a tangled mass of electrical cabling. Air-conditioning ducts snaked their way in and out, carrying away the intense heat generated by all the lighting units and pumping fresh air into the tightly enclosed shooting area. Another important consideration was safety. The drum was constructed with many removable sections, so that people could clamber out quickly in the event of a fire. Victor Lyndon's detailed production notes specified an escape system similar to that of an aircraft, with multiple quick-release panels scattered around the skin of the structure.

It was undoubtedly one of the most impressive and complicated mechanical effects ever devised. (Arthur Clarke joked that MGM's publicity department had typewriters specially adapted to start every page with: 'Never in the history of motion pictures...' when they were describing such wonders.)

Lighting a forty-foot-diameter drum that simply wouldn't stay still was a rigger's nightmare. What's more, Kubrick wanted to make the illumination for the wildly careening set as realistic as possible. In *Dr Strangelove* he had replicated the interior of a B52 bomber to include realistic cabin lights. For *2001*'s centrifuge sequences, strip-lighting diffusers were fitted into recessed panels all around the walls, so as to look like an integral part of the spacecraft interior. Behind each ring of perspex—one for the left wall, one for the right—there was an outer ring of powerful floodlamps, blasting away at full strength. By the time they had shone their way through the semi-transparent panels inside the set, there wasn't much light left to play with. Cameraman Geoffrey Unsworth had to push existing film emulsion to its limits in order to

**The big wheel:**
*The centrifuge set at Borehamwood in 1966, fully illuminated for interior shooting.*

Another view of the centrifuge set, here seen fully illuminated for a shoot. Kubrick's control room, a wood and wire mesh safety cage, can be seen at the bottom left of the picture. He directed from inside, using closed-circuit television and an early form of video recording equipment to help line up the shots.

Notice the fat air-conditioning hose going into the centre of the wheel. Heat would build up inside very quickly under the blazing lights and the air tended to get stuffy.

At roughly 3 o'clock from this view, the HAL 9000 multi-screen panel can be seen, with twelve projectors to provide screen data.

 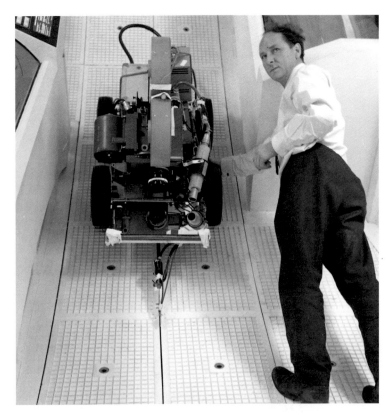

**Rings of light:**
*A close-up of a circular lighting assembly on the centrifuge (above) and camera operator Kelvin Pike with his dolly (top right) climbing the centrifuge's steeply curved floor.*

shoot these scenes. By contrast, the outside of the drum shone like an inferno during takes.

Throughout photography in the 'carousel', film crews had to wear hard hats in order to protect themselves against the bits of stray equipment, forgotten screwdrivers, empty film canisters and so on that fell down from forty feet over their heads as the mammoth construction slowly wheeled about. The customary 'silence' of a take was often interrupted by the popping of exploding light bulbs. There was an incessant tinkling rain of little glass fragments falling out of all kinds of awkward nooks and crannies. There was also an appalling creaking and groaning every time the drum started to turn, as the steel support struts adjusted to the restless motions of their thirty-ton load. And there were powerful electric motors under the rim of the drum, recessed into an expensively bulldozered trench in the studio floor, adding their own unearthly hum.

The principal set-up consisted of a camera bolted rigidly to the floor, with the operator strapped firmly into his chair while he and his camera whirled in a circle. His seat was gimballed like a compass in its mounting, so that the operator could keep his bearings. Meanwhile, the actors stayed at the bottom and 'trod the mill' like hamsters in an exercise wheel, while the set trundled slowly past them. From the camera's point of view—and the audience's—the astronauts appeared to be walking around the walls while the set stood rock steady. It was totally convincing.

For some scenes, one of the actors was strapped securely into place, apparently seated at the kitchenette table. He was sent spinning forty feet into the air. The camera was pointed up at him, but the compositional framing suggested that we were looking 'down' from a considerable height. Then his companion appeared to climb out of a hatch above him and walk 'down' around the rim of the drum, to join him for a meal of squeeze-paste and coffee. In reality, he walked the treadmill until his hapless upside-down colleague span down to meet him at the bottom. Naturally there was no hint on screen of all the safety belts and glued-down breakfasts, and Kubrick deliberately chose camera angles that would intensify the audience's confusion about 'up' and 'down', so that even the most logically-minded among them were dumbfounded by the whole effect when they finally got to see the results.

Other shots were obtained by putting the camera on a wheeled dolly and allowing it to sit at the bottom. Actor Gary Lockwood shadow-boxed just in front of the camera, doing his fitness routine in shorts and tee-shirt. From our point of view, the off-duty spaceman punches and jabs his way around the interior of his little world, while a spectacular procession of computer panels, personal cubicles and deep-freeze compartments rushes past him. All the while, the camera had to be kept about twenty feet ahead of him, some way up the incline of the centrifuge's steeply curving floor. It was held in place by a steel cable fed through a slit in the middle of the floor which sliced its way right around the set. Rubber mats on the floor fell back into place as soon as the cable had snickered through them, so that by the time they were in shot again the cable had left no trace of its passage. All this meant that the drum had to be in two separate halves. The engineering tolerances were extremely fine. Any imbalance would have caused the set to squeeze together at the bottom, thus narrowing the slit, pinching the wire, and perhaps causing the camera to snap off its mounting.

The number of people in the drum had to be kept to a minimum, not just for safety reasons,

but also because of the extreme wide-angle lenses being used in the confined space. Kubrick directed from an office adjacent to the set, using closed-circuit TV. A half-silvered mirror mounted at a slant in front of the camera performed the trick of front-projection in reverse, so that Kubrick's electronic monitoring camera could see precisely the same view. There was also a bulky videotape machine which provided instant, if rather crude 'rushes'. (Kubrick latched on to the potential of video very early on.)

*Shooting in the wheel:*
*Kubrick and his crew line up*
*a shot in the centrifuge.*

***The way in—and out:***
*This shot (above) shows the emergency drop-away hatches all around the centrifuge, which also served as camera ports for low-angle static shots.*

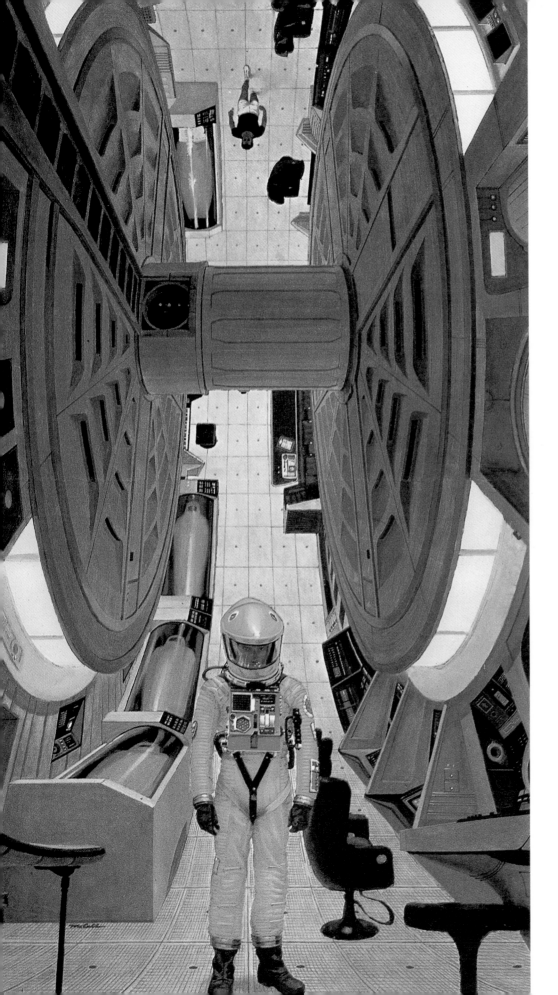

**A home from home:**
Robert McCall's publicity artwork shows Frank Poole standing at the 'bottom' of the centrifuge in his yellow spacesuit. The crew of 'Discovery' would, supposedly, spend most of their time in this topsy-turvy living compartment. Much of that time would be spent unconscious in the hibernation units, which can clearly be seen in this painting.

The rim of the drum was calibrated like the dial of a giant compass. These markings tallied precisely with the various parts of the set inside the drum. Operators on the stage floor controlled the rotation of the drum very carefully, by observing specific sets of instructions to rotate from one calibrated point to another. Meanwhile, the actors inside hit their marks too, using the internal furnishings around them as their guide. This was all to avoid the obvious catastrophe of having cameras and actors falling over, or worse still, on top of each other—for instance, if an actor had tried to hit his mark inside, and the operators on the studio floor had turned the drum too far by mistake. In fact there nearly *was* a catastrophe at one point. A piece of hardware tore loose from its mountings when the camera rig was right up at 12 o'clock high. The object (possibly a projector) smashed down on the floor a few inches from where Gary Lockwood was readying himself for his next scene. If he'd been standing in the wrong place, he would have been in very serious trouble.

The centrifuge was only one of several sets which were built with moving components. There were also sequences demonstrating how the astronauts would move out of the centrifuge and into the non-rotating parts of their ship. The camera was mounted onto the foreground part of the set, while the background section rotated. The actors climbed into the background hatch area, and at the very moment they did so, it stopped spinning—and the *foreground*, along with the camera, started tumbling instead. So of course, it looked as though the astronauts were tumbling about at the far end like washing in a spin-drier. The most important thing was to make the stopping and starting of camera rotation as smooth and subtle as possible.

Earlier shots in the movie, of a stewardess climbing around the walls of the *Aries* kitchen module, were achieved in a similar way. The whole set tumbled, with the camera bolted to it, while she calmly trod the mill.

The principles involved in these effects were physically quite straightforward. Kubrick saw how the laws of physics and a little ingenuity could produce illusions indistinguishable from magic. However, it took precision engineering on a grand scale to produce something that would work in such large and complex interiors. Arthur Clarke's brother, Fred, remembers that the machining and welding on Vickers' elaborate support structure for *Discovery*'s centrifuge was of such fine quality, that 'you could almost imagine they were building a prototype for the real thing.'

The sequences depicting astronauts *outside* the spacecraft were just as convincing. At an early stage in scripting it became obvious that some kind of 'spacewalking' activity would have to be shown. In particular, the scenes depicting the replacement of the AE35 antenna steering unit were crucial to the narrative; besides which, the sheer challenge of depicting people floating apparently quite freely in zero gravity was one which a film of such vaunting ambition could scarcely fail to take up.

Kubrick and his team were determined not to shoot any scenes showing spacemen walking along the hull of their ship in magnetic shoes. This certainly would have been the easy way out, but it wouldn't exactly have been the most exciting or satisfactory portrayal of an 'EVA', although, ironically, magnetic shoes were a favourite option in early spaceflight proposals, until the increasingly lightweight and exotic materials of genuine spacecraft manufacture utterly eliminated the possibility of magnetic steel hulls for spacewalkers to clomp about on. Quite literally, if anybody in *2001* was to be seen apparently floating about on screen, they would have to start out by floating *for real*, in front of the camera, with absolutely no convenient bits of spacecraft skin to stand on, or hold on to. Even when astronauts were to be shown working on the antenna unit, it had to be clear that they were still floating free of the main ship itself. Effects supervisor Wally Veevers was instructed to come up with some method of suspending his actors and stuntmen in mid-air, right there in the studio.

The solution which he and Kubrick finally settled on was ingenious and highly convincing. Like so many of the movie's effects, it was based on painstaking application of a really simple idea. It was also a very hazardous procedure for the various actors and stunt doubles concerned. It was more like performing on a

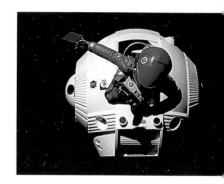

***Out of the back door:*** *Keir Dullea's stunt double emerges from a pod.*

dangerous circus trapeze than moviemaking. A stuntman was suited up, supplied with oxygen bottles and a radio set, and then suspended at great height from the ceiling of the shooting stage by a wire harness. The attachment point on his suit straps lay exactly over his own natural centre of gravity, so he neither tumbled forward, nor backwards, but simply floated like a swimmer. He could kick his arms and legs, but this didn't make him go anywhere, except around in tiny little circles. Without floors or walls to push against, he was as helplessly inert as real spacewalkers are.

The camera was set up directly beneath the suspended stuntman, so that the bulk of his own body concealed the wires behind him. Once everything was lined up, the basic camera angle couldn't be changed, except within fairly tight limits. It always had to be shooting more or less straight up at the roof. (The ceiling was swathed completely, as usual, in vast sheets of black velvet.) The slightest trace of any wires accidentally visible against the brightly coloured spacesuits would have given the game away. Another problem was that the wires tugged at the fabric of the suits, particularly around the attachment points. The resulting creases had to be kept well out of sight.

In order to make it look as though he was being photographed from various different perspectives, the position of the stuntman himself had to be altered, by wiring him up in different ways: sometimes on his belly, sometimes head down, and sometimes on his side. This made it seem as though the camera position was just above him, just below him, right alongside him, or whatever. This was all a very uncomfortable business. The stuntman was often in danger of collapsing from exhaustion or lack of air, or from spending too much time upside-down. It was physically demanding work.

A spectacular shot of an astronaut clambering out of the back door of his pod, and then appearing to float freely away from it, was achieved by putting everything in line above the camera. First the pod was firmly suspended, face up, with its door pointing straight down at the camera. Then the stuntman came tumbling out, hanging from a wire that disappeared inside the pod. From the camera's point of view, this

The picture above shows a pod suspended from the ceiling of a shooting stage at Borehamwood, with a stuntman hanging alongside. The shot below gives some idea of the scale of the operation. A camera and lighting assembly on a dolly sits on special tracks on the floor. The stuntman would be launched from the tall platform.

*Life in the wheel:*
*Keir Dullea in the centrifuge,*
*after climbing down the ladder.*

all seemed to be happening on the straight and level; and audiences had already been taught in previous sequences to think of the pod's doors as being at the back, and not 'underneath'. So they took the apparent right-way-up attitude of the space pod on screen as their visual cue.

Once an astronaut had clambered out of his pod and jetted himself across to the antenna unit, he had to be shown working alongside a piece of spacecraft to the correct scale: lifesize. This required the construction of a very large and detailed portion of *Discovery*'s antenna unit, which then had to be suspended from the ceiling. The scene in the cavernous shooting studio was truly extraordinary at this point, with a spacesuited figure hanging upside down far above the floor, a huge radio dish positioned at an absurdly twisted angle, and everybody trying hard to make sure that the tumbling stuntman didn't swing about too violently and dash his head against it. He was not allowed to hold onto any part of the mock-up, but had to drift alongside it on his wires, mainly upside down, with his limbs aching, his air getting staler and the blood rushing down to his head.

The sequence showing David Bowman's attempt to rescue Frank Poole was particularly demanding on the stuntman concerned. He had to pretend to be a dead body, drifting helplessly in a punctured yellow pressure suit. Curiously enough, he couldn't achieve this illusion by merely doing nothing. He had to keep his arms and legs constantly spreadeagled, and he had to maintain a subtle motion, as his supposedly inert body responded randomly to all the tumbling and gyrating. His wires were suspended from ceiling rails. The camera underneath him was also on tracks, and moved along with him to keep the all-important vertical alignment intact.

On screen, Bowman's pod moves up to him and scoops him up in its manipulator arms. In reality, however, the pod was locked securely into position from struts at the top of the studio, while the stuntman was repeatedly set swinging on his wires until he was able to thud successfully into the waiting arms. All the time, he couldn't betray his aliveness by adjusting his position, or trying to cushion the impact. The finished shot shows the suit's helmet getting a nasty knock. It all looks very sedate, particularly

with the whole thing filmed in slow motion. In fact, the stuntman was colliding at twice the apparent speed on film, not just once, but again and again over many takes.

One final problem that had to be solved was how to create the illusion that astronauts on EVA were indeed operating in the vastness of space. In particular, one shot shows Frank Poole tumbling far off into the void, apparently many hundreds of feet away from us, as he struggles with his severed air hose. Even the largest shooting studio didn't have enough room to accommodate this scale of relative movement between the stuntman and the camera.

So how was it done? The stuntman was given a gentle shove, to set him spinning like a top at the end of his wire—though, of course, he still held his station right above the camera. He clutched at his broken hose, as though in a panic. This was established as a 'master' shot. For the final sequence it was pro-cessed as a positive, and then projected onto a square of highly reflective white card. Then, another camera was able to back away from this con-siderably less-than-lifesize image, apparently to infinity; but it only had to track back a few feet, rather than across half a mile. Motion across the screen was also obtained in this way, but with the camera moving from side to side relative to the image on the card, rather than backwards and forwards. The same principle in reverse

allowed a careening empty pod to hurtle towards us from what seemed to be many hun-dreds of feet into the scene, as Hal throws away the murder weapon, so to speak. The tumbling asteroids are another example of how a sense of almost limitless distance was obtained within the walled confines of Borehamwood.

Some interior sequences also demanded the illusion of weightlessness. When David Bowman is forced to blow his way into an airlock, the same wire harness technique was used. The corridor set appears to the viewer to be receding into the screen. In fact, the set was built vertically. Keir Dullea was suspended from the open hatch at the top, and was hauled up and down on his harness. Speeding up the sequence during the edit added an appropriate mood of panic. From our perspective, it looks as though Dullea is crashing backwards and forwards, not up and down.

The scene in Hal's brain room also required Dullea to hang from a wire. Again, Kubrick shot the scene as though the brain room were lying on its side; but the huge set, three storeys high, was built vertically. The danger of these sequences was highlighted by the misfortune of a rigger who fell from the top of the set and injured his back. Dullea has said that Kubrick was the only director he would ever have con-sidered risking his life for, hanging about on thin wires from such heights.

**Rotating takes:**
*The entire lunar shuttle kitchen set rotated, in a manner similar to the centrifuge, so that the stewardess could appear to walk upside-down.*

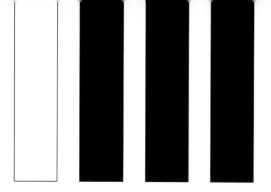

# 8: a very private man

THROUGHOUT Kubrick's career, promoters of the *auteur* theory of film-making were fascinated by his ability to achieve genuine 'authority' over his own work. He was a rare director whose big, expensive films could be likened to works of art issuing from a single creative talent. Of course Kubrick relied on the usual collaborative army of co-screenwriters, technicians, designers and so forth but, with the exception of *Spartacus*, the final shape of all his films lay within his own judgement. There were no script committees, no market analysts. Nobody was allowed to interfere. Kubrick was powerful enough to wield total control over his own output. Any director working today will tell you that this must have been a privileged and unusual circumstance. Perhaps above all of Kubrick's projects, *2001: A Space Odyssey* emerged as the most expensive personal 'art film' ever made.

So how did he enforce his vision? People said that he wore out Hollywood executives by the dozen. He didn't get ulcers, he gave 'em. The escalating budget for *2001* was a case in point. As Keith Hamshere says, 'It was all down to Stanley keeping MGM off his back. He was controlling the control freaks. I've never seen anything like that since, and I'll never see it again.' Roger Caras's assistant Ivor Powell often came across Kubrick on the phone to MGM in America. 'He'd tell them how wonderful everything was, and then he'd get off the phone and say to Victor Lyndon, "Send them three minutes of centrifuge footage." He fed MGM snippets of the film, piecemeal, to keep them distracted. It was always just enough so that they would see that something really good was happening, but never enough for them to understand how the movie as a whole was shaping up.'

Inevitably, MGM executives would call Kubrick's bluff now and then, arriving at Borehamwood with dark expressions on their faces. According to Arthur Clarke, they sometimes muttered about Stanley perhaps being kind enough to let them have *2001* in time for a release in 2002. Warned of their impending visits, Kubrick would summon his junior assistants. 'Guys, it's a raid! Make up some more charts and plans for the walls here. Let's blind 'em with science.' Powell would mock up serious-looking material purporting to illustrate obscure administrative aspects of the production. 'Then the suits would turn up and ask, "What do all these charts mean?" Knowing Stanley as I did, I always had some kind of an answer prepared. He liked people who could anticipate the unexpected.'

'Occasionally I witnessed some friction between Kubrick and the studio over the movie taking too long and costing too much,' says Trumbull. 'There'd be periodic showdowns where MGM would turn up and want to look at the sets or see some footage. Kubrick kept that

**Kubrick in command:**
*Here he directs Gary Lockwood in the pod cockpit set*

very private. He didn't involve us in any upsetting political machinations and we were very protected from it. When you think about it, originally I was supposed to be on the film for nine months, and I ended up there for more than two years, so the whole thing must have been a strain for MGM.'

Not that Kubrick was trying to hide any kind of recklessness with MGM's money—far from it. Dan Richter, who now runs a computerized payroll service for the film industry, is well qualified to place Kubrick's reputation as a big

Hamshere says 'I was too young to worry about budgets. I just thought this must be normal for the film business, although people would sometimes turn and say to me "This must be costing a fortune!" But we never really talked too much about money. Stanley always said we should just do whatever was right for the film.'

Stills photographer John Jay remembers how strange the financial environment surrounding *2001* seemed to him. 'I would go to the production office claiming for a pad of paper and a box of pencils, and they'd say "What!" And next

**Eyes like two black olives:** *Stanley Kubrick's intense gaze beams out from behind a mass of camera equipment*

spender in context: 'The truth is, he didn't spend nearly as much money as most people in Hollywood. Today a huge chunk of the money just goes on hiring star actors. Also, Stanley didn't pay his crew too much. He was fairly frugal, and he hired lots of young people, who were enthusiastic, full of energy and also very cheap because they hadn't yet earned their spurs in the industry. *2001* was an unusually complex film, which is why it cost so much by 1960s' standards, but the money all ended up on screen, not in people's pockets.'

day I would put in a requisition for the latest camera, specially flown in from Germany or wherever, and there wouldn't be the slightest fuss. Stanley would say "Whatever you need." Three days later it would be delivered to my office. If it was a frippery, you didn't get it, but if you could justify it, you got whatever you wanted, regardless of cost.'

Kubrick's finance director Ronnie Bear was always on people's backs. MGM would have been impressed. Even in Africa, shooting the *Dawn of Man* plates, Andrew Birkin was hounded, via telex, to deliver proper accounts of his every last expense. 'Dear Andrew, I was horrified at your recent request for an additional $3,000 without proper itemization. I am also in receipt of your last set of accounts, which you claim as amounting to $2,547. The equipment items I understand. However you specify $22 'entertainment' on March 8 for three people. Please list the names of those people. Best regards, R. Bear.'

On his return to London, an exhausted Birkin took a cab from the airport to his flat in Chelsea, dropped off his luggage while the cab waited, and then went to Borehamwood. A few days later, Bear dropped him a note. 'I was most concerned to receive your taxi bill for $15. We could have hired a Rolls Royce for that price.'

Looking at *2001* today, there's no doubting that Kubrick delivered MGM excellent value for their money. Even if he did keep them waiting.

The real enigma of Kubrick was this: nobody who was ever held hypnotized by him can quite explain how he did it. Laurie Barr at Master Models remembers his brief contact with Kubrick thus: 'He was very quiet, he didn't say much to me. But you had this overwhelming sense of a mind at work behind those eyes. Some people loved him, and some people absolutely hated his guts, but everybody held him in absolute awe, no question about it.' Keir Dullea echoes the sentiment. 'He had this quiet sense of himself that ultimately spoke of great power. You always felt it.'

According to Richter, 'Stanley always made sure he knew more than the other person. That's a very powerful thing to have on your side. If he was talking to biologists about apeman behaviour, or discussing astronomy with Carl Sagan, he would always bring as much to the meeting as the experts. He would read all the literature and do the work.'

Alexander Walker has written 'Just how Kubrick exerted his willpower, it's hard to say. He didn't let himself be worn out. He wore out others.' Ken Adam is a case in point. He designed the War Room for *Dr Strangelove*, and was disappointed when circumstances prevented him from working on *2001*. He did meet Kubrick to discuss this possibility, but by then the director had already been working for six months with Tony Masters and his team. Ken

***An objective intellect:***
*Kubrick on the space station set. Unlike many directors, he preferred to remain calm when faced by technical crises.*

**Gary Lockwood:**
*'With Stanley, anything could happen at almost any time. There were an infinite number of ways he might approach things.'*

Adam had more or less missed the boat. On *Dr Strangelove*, Adam had reworked the War Room design countless times, until he was all but on the point of despair. Somehow, his boss was never quite satisfied with it. Eventually Adam made a design which Kubrick liked, but the brilliant production designer felt he had pushed himself harder to reach this final result than ever before. (Harry Lange experienced something similar. Kubrick commented to him, 'You never know what you might be capable of, if you don't try.') In an interview with Michel Ciment, Ken Adam suggested that he became a more flexible designer after *Strangelove*. Many other collaborators have also acknowledged that Kubrick had a knack of bringing out the best from the people around him.

Poor Ken Adam also had a chance to bring out Kubrick's wickedly dry sense of humour, as Arthur Clarke once gleefully recalled. On his visit to Kubrick to discuss *2001*, Adam turned up in his pride and joy, a shiny new Jaguar motor car, 1965's smartest and very latest model. Stanley looked the car over coolly, and said 'Ken, seriously, if money were no object, what would you really have bought yourself?'

A few years later, Adam would return for more punishment, designing Kubrick's *Barry Lyndon* (1975). He got through it mainly by living on tranquillizers. But working with Kubrick generally turned out to be a huge adventure for those who could take the pace. The British technicians at work in Borehamwood on *2001* soon learned to respect their director's absolute mastery over the whole production. It is perfectly fair to say that, despite his medium height, shy nature and quiet voice, he held several hundred people around him in thrall—and film people like nothing better than a director who is sure of what he wants, even if he won't tolerate anything that falls anywhere short. Roger Caras says, 'You never knew what Stanley was really like until you saw him up to his armpits in gadgets and sets and people. It was awesome.'

People weren't quite so much impressed by Kubrick's odd sense of timekeeping and his fondness for working late into the night. This was seldom a problem for his rank-and-file technicians, union-protected carpenters and so forth, but it could be a considerable bane to his senior collaborators. At four o'clock in the morning, for instance, Kubrick might well be awake and experimenting with new ideas which he would immediately wish to discuss with them, much to their chagrin. They would sometimes be woken by his telephone calls in the pre-dawn darkness. Clarke, in particular, found this harrowing. 'I have an absolute rule. No sane person is up before nine in the morning, and no law-abiding one after ten at night.' Stanley's clock ran out of phase with Clarke's—and everyone else's. Editor Ray Lovejoy says, 'He was very appreciative of what you did, but he wanted you to work 24 hours a day.'

According to Derek Cracknell's assistant, Richard Jenkins, the unionized staff would assemble at about five o'clock every evening to vote on whether or not to work overtime that day. Kubrick would watch, expectantly, as the majority of hands shot up in a 'yes' vote. 'But I had just got married, and we were struggling with our first baby, and I usually wanted to get home, so I would vote "No". And Stanley would glower at me across the table. But the reason we put up with it is we all knew he was pushing himself even harder.'

'That was another reason why Stanley liked hiring young people,' says Richter. 'On the whole, they didn't have families to go home to, and they could work all day and into the night.'

Having a family was no protection, however. Tony Masters' wife Heather recalls 'Tony never got back home before ten at night. And when he did, the phone was often going. I didn't see him at all for two years.' But Kubrick was no monster. Heather also remembers that when her young son had croup, he ordered an expensive inhaler to be flown in from America. She thought this was very kind and has always been grateful. 'Stanley was a lovely, very sweet man, which people who didn't know him don't often realize.' For Kubrick, collector of information, gatherer of data, perhaps that inhaler simply represented the logical answer to the problem at hand? Maybe, but his affection towards his own children, and the large numbers of cats and dogs which constantly surrounded him at home, testified to a conventionally humane man with a rich family life. Accounts of his many kindnesses to actors and collaborators didn't find their way quite so often into magazine and newspaper stories as did the wildly exaggerated tales of errant genius. 'Oh, people are always writing such nonsense about him. They don't have the faintest idea', Heather says—and Con Pederson echoes her sentiments. 'He was a generous man, and surprisingly folksy. People in Hollywood didn't know him very well, but working with him for two or three years at a stretch was a very special experience.'

Perfectionism is another theme that keeps cropping up every time talk turns to the subject of Kubrick. According to Hamshere, there was a well-worn joke doing the rounds at Borehamwood by late 1967. 'In six days, God created the heavens and the earth. On the seventh day, Stanley sent everything back for modifications.' A photo of him was pinned on the wall of the art department, with a scribbled caption: 'Okay, guys, what do we do on day eight?'

After the Creation of any Kubrickean universe, there was *always* a 'day eight'. Jenkins tells of the sequence where a stewardess (played by Edwina Carroll) walks upside-down in the Aries lunar shuttle kitchen: 'We shot it time after time

for a week, and every next morning Stanley would view the rushes, which always looked fantastic, but there'd always be something he didn't like that none of the rest of us even noticed. At last the day came when the scene was absolutely flawless. And Stanley said, "That's it! That's great! We'll shoot it this afternoon." It just went on and on.'

According to Bruce Logan, primarily responsible for the HAL readout displays, 'Stanley threw out most of the first six months of effects work except for those readouts, and we began again. Unmanned NASA probes were starting to send back pictures of the lunar surface, and the reality was different to the miniature landscapes that we'd already been working with. Stanley insisted that we had to take that into account.'

Many stories about Kubrick concern this ceaseless obsession with total quality. Dullea says, 'One day we were ready to shoot the first centrifuge scenes and Stanley said he didn't like

*Keir Dullea:*
*'I think he made his movies in England so that he could keep as far away as possible from the Hollywood hierarchy. I truly admired his independence.'*

**On the moon:**
*Kubrick directs the lunar
scenes (above & left).*

# a director at work

**Mulling it over:**
*Kubrick ponders a
problem in the 'Aries'
passenger deck set.*

our boots. We didn't shoot during that entire day, while the boot problem was fixed.' And Harry Lange's wife Daisy remembers that she and several other production unit wives and girlfriends spent days creating information panels and locker numbers from Letraset to embellish obscure pieces of the spacecraft sets. On camera, the tiny lettering would register as little more than a smudge, but Kubrick wanted realism at the smallest scale, just in case.

Kubrick's desire for control extended well beyond the duration of a shoot or the release of a film. 'One day I was walking towards Stage 3 at Borehamwood,' recalls Pederson, 'And I saw this airplane that someone was planning to use on some other movie. I saw Stanley later that day and I said, "That plane out there looks like the bomber in *Dr Strangelove*." So we ran over to Stage 3 and Stanley stared at the plane and said, "Oh my God!" He freaked, and from that point on he had this slash-and-burn policy of destroying sets and models so that they couldn't be used in other movies. Today I guess those props would be celebrities in their own right, but at the time we didn't think about pre-serving them. He was just trying to stop them turning up later in some vastly inferior movie.'

And during *2001*'s release in Europe, Kubrick organized for Andrew Birkin to slip into the major European cinemas and photograph the screen while the film was playing—just to be absolutely sure that the projection systems were up to scratch. Significantly, the only time Birkin ever blotted his copybook with Stanley was when he rescued an early draft of *2001*'s script, complete with the director's handwritten notes,

**At the controls:**
*Kubrick tries out the buttons on an instrument panel (above) and surveys the scene in the pod bay set (below). No detail is too small to be checked by the director in person.*

from the wastebasket. He gave it to the British Film Institute, and a few weeks later their magazine *Sight and Sound* announced how proud the Institute was to have received such a fascinating item into their collection. Kubrick called Birkin. 'One day, I'm sure you'll become a great director or a writer. And then you'll realize you don't want people seeing your first drafts.'

Birkin's many trips to the cinema gave Kubrick a chance to check on a final task he'd given to effects technician Bruce Logan just before release. 'Our effects shots were as close to first-generation as possible in every instance. Stanley realized that, for foreign releases of the film, when it came to the *2001: A Space Odyssey* title card in the first few frames, the words on screen would have to be translated into the relevant languages. He ordered us to create the background sunrise effect as fresh footage for every translation the movie was slated for, so that it wouldn't simply be copied and recopied every time the film went to a different country. Long after everyone else at Borehamwood had packed up and gone home, I was shooting seven exactly similar versions of that opening, all onto fresh film.'

An early associate of Kubrick's, James B. Harris, has defended the director's protective attitude to his work and legacy: 'Once the movie is finished, everyone else leaves, and he is left alone with his footage forever.'

Kubrick seldom lost his temper on set. His method of demonstrating dissatisfaction was much subtler than that. A technician at work on a particularly complicated shot on *2001* kept getting something wrong, despite the director's calm and reassuring efforts to steer him in the right direction. Eventually Kubrick just said, very quietly, 'Look, if you don't want to do this my way, you may as well go home.' Next take, the shot was perfect.

A young designer, Tony Pratt, helped create the space pod concepts. He prepared a full-size mock-up for Kubrick's inspection. The spherical model was just a rough version, made from plywood, more or less held together with sticky tape, but it gave a good impression of the proposed capsule's general layout. It sat in the middle of a cavernous studio at Borehamwood,

the vast space empty for the last few days before the set builders moved in. Tony felt a little nervous as Kubrick arrived at the appointed hour: 'Okay—what have you got for me?' At this awkward moment the sticky tape fell apart, and the pod disintegrated before Kubrick's eyes. Long, ghastly seconds passed. Tony wanted to sink into the floor.

'I'll come back and look at it another time', Kubrick said softly, and walked out.

On another occasion, after five hours spent setting up a shot, Kubrick found his sound recordist apologizing to him that, unfortunately, the mikes weren't quite ready. He'd done his setting up in the first hour or so, but hadn't felt the need to check his usually perfectly reliable gear since then. When you worked for Stanley Kubrick, you didn't make dangerous assumptions like that. The entire studio was braced for a justifiable blast of directorial fury. Once again, Kubrick showed how a deep calm could be a far more effective tool of authority. Quietly, almost in a whisper, he said: 'The next time I have a five-hour camera rehearsal, perhaps you might think of getting your sound problems solved in the same period of time?' Then he looked at his watch and said to everybody, 'We might as well break for the day.' Needless to say, the sound man was thoroughly prepared by the next time he came face-to-face with his director.

If you didn't give him what he wanted, he pushed—gently, often kindly—but pushed nevertheless, until you delivered. And sometimes, in the pressure of the moment, he would fire people. Birkin says, 'A director needs to establish authority over a huge team of people, and sometimes a little blood has to be let, to prove that you're not going to be messed around.' Maybe Kubrick was a little hasty at times. Logan seemed for a while to be a Kubrick favourite, until one day 'he was looking at some rushes—he was a tough audience—and because I was on nightshift that time, I wasn't able to defend myself at the morning rushes. So I got fired. But within a week he rang me and asked me to come back. I said that he'd better double my salary, and he graciously agreed, and apart from that one incident we always got along very well. Stanley was, on the one hand, one of the most demanding people I've ever met, but on the other hand, also one of the most generous.'

Some people cracked. A freelance artist, sculpting models of the lunar surface for 2001, reworked them again and again, meeting each time with Kubrick's terse disapproval. He left the studio lot in tears. Nor was his the only creative temperament practically traumatized by his 2001 experience. Film composer Alex North was at the edge of nervous collapse by the time Kubrick had finished with him, not least because the director dumped all his specially com-missioned work in favour of existing orchestral recordings. Rough justice? Ask the film critics. Nine times out of ten, they will tell you about Kubrick's 'absolutely brilliant use of music'.

North had worked perfectly well with Kubrick on *Spartacus*, and it seems to have been MGM's idea that the composer should be hired for 2001—although Kubrick made the formal approach to North, asking him to come aboard. When the New York-based composer arrived in London in December 1967 to discuss the score, Kubrick warned him, politely, that some of the 'temporary' Strauss working tracks that he'd been using during the initial editing phase might be retained. He tended to prefer existing music over original film scores, because he would know, in advance, what he was getting. North said that he would rather create entirely fresh music. True to form, Kubrick installed North in a luxurious London apartment in Chelsea, and showered him with every conceivable aide to his work: tape recorders, stereo decks and a concert-standard piano.

But Kubrick had been delving into his large private record collection right from the start of 2001's production, and in the end, he preferred his selections from Strauss and Katchaturian, and the atonal choral experiments of Ligeti to North's music. The composer recalled in a 1992 interview with *Cinefantastique* magazine, 'I thought, this is the end. I've had it. It was really one of the biggest disappointments in my career. Kubrick never apologized.' Before North came aboard, Frank Cordell, a British com-poser, was also caught in the Kubrick mangler, and even Ligeti complained when Kubrick distorted some of his music for the climactic hotel room scenes of 2001. But nothing

whatsoever—including the dismissal of North's entire score and the threat of a lawsuit from Ligeti—was allowed to interfere with the director's particular vision of how a film should look or sound.

On the set of 2001, that included unions and other irrelevant constructs of the society that surrounded him. There were a few work-to-rules and other minor rebellions, but resistance soon crumbled. The main area of contention was that Kubrick's appreciation of unionized lines of demarcation was rather unorthodox. Division of labour among technicians is usually adhered to fairly strictly in the film world, but he would often set competing teams from apparently unrelated departments to work on similar problems. After many months on this complex film, people soon settled down to the inevitable: at some stage, almost everybody would be involved in almost everything. Kubrick wasn't going to listen to any interdepartmental gripes. All he cared about was that whatever idea was put in front of him, and wherever it had come from, it had to *work* (hence the tension between Brian Johnson and Wally Veevers over the centrifuge projectors, for

*A cordial relationship: Kubrick and Unsworth stare thoughtfully into the monitor relaying pictures from inside the centrifuge set.*

instance). Kubrick had absolutely no qualms about asking several different people at once to come up with solutions to a problem, whereupon he would select the one he liked best and discard the rest. Inevitably, a great deal of time, money and effort went into creating procedures, models and effects which never made it into the final cut of the film.

One result of this unusually interdisciplinary working environment has been that, thirty-odd years after the fact, almost everybody discussing those days takes credit for having devised almost everything, and they may well be justified in doing so. Another outcome was that the screen credits sometimes bear little relation to people's actual contributions to the film.

Kubrick wasn't too concerned with the exact definition of his own role, either (except when it came to credits). Though nominally the director, he would happily—indeed, insistently—throw himself into every aspect of production. He edited the footage, adapted the soundtrack, selected the music, pulled focus on the camera, lit the sets, and chose the fabric for his actors' costumes. Then he checked with his publicity department that film stills for the press releases were set in the right kind of slide mounts. Then he proof-read all the advance brochures...

And if Stanley said he wanted to hand-hold a giant 65mm camera, then he damn well would. Dullea says 'That scene where I was climbing up to the HAL brain room was hand-held by Stanley himself. He knew every bit as much about camerawork as Geoff Unsworth, our principal cameraman.'

Kubrick often shot hand-held takes, particularly when he was trying to evoke an unsteady, subjective viewpoint. For the scene showing astronauts descending a ramp to confront the lunar Monolith, he wanted to convey a jittery feeling through the camerawork. After all, one might expect a spaceman's knees to be buckling slightly at the prospect of such a strange encounter. For this shot, it wasn't possible to get away with any drop in image quality, so there was no question of switching to a smaller camera format. Kubrick devised a method of manhandling a 65mm Mitchell camera, with grips and assistants helping him to support the weight while he trod carefully down

**Moon men in white coats:**
*Kubrick and his 'lunar scientists' survey the huge Tycho crater excavation set at Shepperton on the morning of December 29, 1965. This was the very first day of shooting.*

the ramp, closely trailing his silver-suited actors. He wanted the shot a certain way, and he got it.

Kubrick's relationship with Geoffrey Unsworth was perfectly cordial. Unsworth wisely chose to bite his lip when confronted by his latest fascination—using instant Polaroid film to check exposure and lighting, over and above the traditional photo-electric light meters and f-stop calculation charts. However, when it came to Kubrick's unquenchable conviction that monochrome Polaroid of a certain sensitivity could precisely match the exposure characteristics of the colour film in the Panavision movie camera, some stories differ. It seems Unsworth wasn't averse to quietly slipping the f-stop notch on the Panavision lens back to his preferred exposure once Stanley had finished fidgeting with his Polaroids. Nowadays, studio photographers regard instant film as a standard tool for checking their set-ups. As so often, Kubrick was somewhat further ahead of his contemporaries in his assessment of the latest new toy on the market.

Even *approaching* a camera can be an unusual thing for a director to do. Russell Metty, principal cameraman on *Spartacus*, was very surprised to find the young Kubrick looking through the camera and setting up shots. He told Kubrick that most directors simply barked out general instructions, 'Russell, I want a wide shot here, a close-up there, come in tight on that', before disappearing into their trailers. Kubrick's instinct as a photographer was always to handle the camera himself.

And instinct *was* an important consideration in Kubrick's directorial style. For such an intellectual man, for someone so keen on the disciplines of careful preparation, risk prevention and the gathering of total information, this might seem surprising: that he felt his way through much of his work, rather than relying purely on rational thought. 'The style of any film has more to do with intuition than with analysis', he told French film author Michel Ciment. And of *2001* in particular, he once said 'Sometimes the truth of a thing is not so much in the think of it, but in the feel of it.' This accounted for his antipathetic attitude towards film scripts, and left him free to make sudden leaps of imagination. He planned everything down to the last detail but never allowed himself to become creatively crippled or tied down by his own super-organization. Gary Lockwood puts it well: 'Stanley was simply much more intelligent than other directors, in a non-linear way. He considered things from a broader perspective and you found that anything could happen at almost any time. Despite all the careful preparations, he designed *2001* with an air of flexibility, and that's what made the picture brilliant.'

'He was an extraordinary filmmaker,' says Con Pederson. 'I once asked him, somewhat stupidly, how he thought Alfred Hitchcock or some other director would have done something we were discussing, and he said, "How would I know? I've never seen anyone else direct." And that was a good point. He taught himself how to make films. I also asked him why he ended up producing all the time, and he said, "You'll never find a producer who can read your mind." So he was a micro-manager at every level, but I never had a problem with that. We got along great.' Pederson, in fact, was amazed that Kubrick could find the energy for directing and producing. 'Believe it or not, directing is not always a creative position. I think unpredictability is a big part of art, but directing is all about management of human relations, logistics, details and so on. On top of all that, Stanley still found room for a kind of danger—even a kind of bravery or recklessness. He was always trying things where there was a high risk of failure. But he wasn't this obstinate solitary genius of popular imagination. He needed people to bounce off, and he would often turn around and ask if he was doing the right thing.'

Andrew Birkin remembers Kubrick playing a very scratched record of *The Blue Danube* when he and everyone else became bored with checking special effects rushes day after day in interminable silence. Gradually habituated to the tune, Kubrick turned to his colleagues one morning and said, with a gleam in his eye, 'Wait a minute. Could we actually use this for real? Am I crazy, or would it be a stroke of genius?'

He kept his eyes and ears open to the people around him, and absorbed everything he saw and heard. No matter what subjects cropped up in apparently casual conversation, he would always find something of usefulness in the chatter. John Hoesli remembers the Hal brain room set was dizzyingly high, and Kubrick was a little reluctant to go up to the top of it (he didn't like heights and from the 1960s onwards never flew, despite his pilot's licence). He turned to Hoesli and said, 'The top hatch—is it insert-worthy? Maybe somebody'd better go up and check it.' The phrase 'insert-worthy' was Kubrick's current jargon for 'Is it good enough to go on camera?' Hoesli shrugged his shoulders, said 'Hold on a minute,' and ran off to fetch his director a pair of powerful binoculars... Kubrick had the good grace to laugh heartily at this. A year later he was using those same binoculars to check focus on his giant front-projection screen.

Idle banter was not a significant factor in Kubrick's conversations, however. Even his jokes frequently had something to do with handling the work colleagues around him or testing their mettle. As far as outsiders were concerned, he was reluctant to grant interviews, hated to be quoted, and seldom committed himself to paper, which is a pity, since he was as inventive and creative in conversation as he was on film. Only a very few privileged journalists ever got to see him. He would select good, trusted writers and speak through them. He would never be found doing the rounds, trotting out the same old stories again and again to different media hacks on different days. He didn't give press conferences. Alexander Walker, a critic who counted Kubrick as a friend, has lamented that 'Before the world became so bothersome to him, it was possible to meet him quite easily.' Kubrick would have argued that his reluctance to move in the outside world had nothing to do with antipathy on his part. It's simply that he was much too busy getting on with his work.

And it's best not to describe this work as an *oeuvre*. He was wary of film theory, of the endless verbiage his films attracted in the arty magazines. Throughout the few interviews he gave in connection with *2001*, he demonstrated a marked reluctance to provide an interpretation of his own work. 'I tried to create a visual experience, one that bypasses verbalized pigeonholing and directly penetrates the subconscious,' he told his *Playboy* interviewer in

1968. (*Playboy* published one of the lengthiest and most worthwhile interviews ever granted by Kubrick on the subject of *2001* and his fascination for science and space.)

The challenge was, of course, for the independently-minded Kubrick to carry along hundreds of people around him in the studio, so that they could transform his intangible 'subconscious' mental images into physical constructs. This wasn't always easy, especially when he hoarded so much of a project's pattern largely in his head. Giving him what he wanted could be difficult when, inevitably, you didn't have access to his personal interior vision. This is why so many shots were redone, so many designs reworked again and again, till something emerged that was equivalent to that secret pattern inside his head. He employed the physical and creative labours of vast technical armies in studios the size of aircraft hangars, and solicited advice from fellow film makers around the world, but in essence he still needed to work like a writer or a painter tucked safely away in a garret, scribbling and scratching away until the poem is just right, the delicate sketch just so. 'You won't find a producer who can read your mind', as he told Pederson. According to Logan, 'Stanley once told me how great it would be if he could make films without having to use people. I think he was about ninety per cent serious.'

Why did people stand for it? Why did experienced, self-respecting artists, writers and technicians with their own perfectly valid creative agendas flock to work with him? 'Stanley had this infectious energy', Lange explains. 'You just got carried along by his incredible enthusiasm. He had a great capacity for making you believe in what he was doing. You learned a hell of a lot from him. A lot of people owe their entire careers to Stanley.'

'Oh, everybody wanted to work with him,' says Brian Johnson. He makes that assertion sound self-evident. 'He was a very unusual man, to put it bluntly. Mind you, Ridley Scott can be quite a handful, and Terry Gilliam too, but it's really worthwhile to work with them. I think the best directors probably have to be a bit crazy to get the job done, because it takes an unusual

kind of determination to make a film that's any good, instead of just average. They've got to have the ideas, then find the money, then they've got to keep the studios off their backs, and then run a crew of, maybe, hundreds of people. Now, that's definitely not a job for an ordinary sort of person.'

Dullea says, 'Kubrick was immensely supportive. I loved working with him. For the emergency airlock scene, I was dropping from the top of the set with nothing but a circus stunt specialist on the other end of a thin wire to break my fall. I wouldn't have risked my life in that way for any other director.'

Albeit at slightly less risk, art director John Hoesli felt similarly driven, though he has some difficulty finding the right words to explain himself. 'Stanley inspired people. I can't really tell you how, but he had this knack of making people do that little bit more. Even the office boy!' (That 'office boy' was Tony Frewin, a 17-year-old runner on the *2001* set who became Kubrick's assistant for many years.) Hoesli is capable of talking non-stop about his work on *2001*: 'That film represents some very important pages in the story of my life.' On the subject of Kubrick, he expresses a familiar sentiment: 'Oh, a marvellous man. Marvellous. A genius. Incredibly clever.'

But occasionally difficult to work with?

'Oh, yes. He could be very frustrating. He'd drive you absolutely crazy, but you just put up with it. You see, Stanley had these very piercing dark eyes, like two little black olives. You couldn't flannel him. He'd see right through you in an instant. But if you were straight with him, he was fine. I remember once, he was barraging me with endless questions about the detailing on the hibernation system, and I just had to shout out in mid-stream, "Look, Stanley, I don't know! But just give me half an hour and I'll find out." And that was fine with him. But you couldn't ever pull a fast one on him.'

Hoesli recalls meeting Kubrick for the first time in New York, when the director asked him if he'd read the script yet. 'Well, I hadn't, but I tried to bluff it and said, yes, I'd taken a quick look at it. So Stanley started asking me these increasingly detailed, specific questions, and I got more and more lost. But he kept coming at me, very quietly. He knew I was flannelling him, and he knew that I knew he knew... I was always very straight with him after that.'

Johnson recalls this knack of Stanley's only too well. 'You gave him the benefit of your expertise, but suddenly you'd see a glint in his eye—like, "Aha! I've *got* you!" And he would know, with uncanny precision, to ask the one question that you didn't have an answer for. And you'd hesitate for a fatal moment, and he'd say "Brian? Just answer me, 'yes' or 'no.'" He was always happy with an honest answer, good or bad, but a lot of people in the movie business just say what they think a director wants to hear, and he didn't like that.'

Passing him in a corridor, or sharing a cup of coffee and a sandwich with him in a rare quiet moment, it was easy sometimes, but usually wrong, to confuse his quiet-spoken manner with indifference. 'You'd try to speak to him about ordinary everyday stuff, and he'd just seem to ignore you,' Johnson recalls, 'but it was just this way he had, unless you were dealing with something very specific to the movie. Anyway, I was quite interested in flying at that time, and I mentioned it in passing to Stanley because, you know, he used to fly till he gave it up. No comment! Just looked down at the floor and walked off. So, anyway, just when I thought I wasn't anywhere on his horizon, you know, a non-entity beneath his consideration, this great pile of aviation magazines turned up on my desk one day with a note from him. "You might find these useful." I was very touched, to be honest, that he'd gone to that kind of trouble.'

'Stanley was a genius,' Roger Caras says, as though that were explanation in itself. Though he warns 'Geniuses—and I've known maybe five or six in my life, and I include Arthur in this—well, they have a monster inside of them that's eating them alive, and that's their frontal lobes. They must feed this thing constantly, and they can't tolerate boredom. That's what drives them to yet greater depths of understanding, of digging.'

Caras remembers a revealing incident on the *Dawn of Man* set. For an entire morning, technicians had been milling around the projection system, trying to line it up accurately with the screen. A millimetre out of position, and the resulting image would go out of focus. Try

as they might, they couldn't get it sharp. Kubrick watched for a while, and then very quietly said, 'I think the mirror's on the wrong way round. Or else the transparency.' His technicians eagerly assured him that everything had been double-checked. Nope, the problem was with the alignment, and it would take them a while yet to fix. Several hours later, the problem hadn't gone away. Kubrick patiently repeated his assertion: 'The transparency must be the wrong way around.' It was such a simple problem, nobody else could believe that it might be the cause of so much difficulty. But it was. The image on the transparency was beaming its way through the thin layer of glass that backed the film emulsion, and the tiny degree of blurring was showing up on the big screen.

While the stage floor swarmed with technicians, all wielding screwdrivers and tape measures, Kubrick never once found the need to fiddle with the mechanisms of the projector itself. According to Caras, 'He never touched a thing. He just stood there and thought the problem through, as if contemplating a chess problem.'

And what of the director's famous reputation for reclusiveness? 'He loved the fact that, in England, he didn't have to carry any ID in his pockets', Logan remembers. 'Stanley was basically secretive, a very private person', Caras explains. 'He was tolerant and unassuming. He didn't lord it over others, but understanding something twenty minutes before anybody else in the room did, and having an incredible memory that probed to unbelievable depths when he was interested in something—that tended to make Stanley seem quiet and reserved unless you knew him well. But he had a really wonderful sense of humour when he was relaxed with someone—and, of course, he had this absolutely insatiable curiosity.'

But 'reserved' is too simplistic a word to describe Kubrick's relationship with the outside world. 'He was great to be around,' says Richter. 'He loved to look at every possibility, to try things countless different ways. He was always open to your suggestions. You'd have one idea, and he'd bounce off you and come up with a hundred more. The older movie professionals found his approach difficult, because they were fixed in their ways. They thought they knew how certain things were supposed to be done. The only time I ever saw Stanley get angry was with people whose minds were closed. That's another reason why young people did the lion's share of the work on *2001*.'

'Stanley is technical. He loves talking about the gadgets, but he's also wonderful with actors,' says Dullea. 'I've always heard that he's not an actor's director, but that doesn't make sense. When actors just don't get it, I suppose that's when conflict arises, but I believe that, as a performer, you have an obligation to try and understand what he wants, and then deliver it.' It's November 1999, and Dullea still can't help but think of Kubrick in the present tense.

In 1985 Simon Davis, one of the apemen from *2001*, worked with Kubrick on *Full Metal Jacket* as costume designer, this time under his real name, Keith Denny. 'It was the end of the day, with the sun going down, and the light was absolutely perfect. Stanley asked two of his actors to walk towards the camera, nice and natural, with this fantastic light in the background. But they were over-tired from a long shoot, or whatever. Anyway, they started fooling around. They just wouldn't take the route that he wanted. "Come on guys, just walk the way I asked you. It's not complicated." He wasn't angry. He just sounded quietly disappointed that no one else could see the shot that he saw. No one else cared enough to try and get it. Like I say, he didn't lose his temper, but as he turned around, I swear there was a tear in the corner of his eye. Stanley *cares*, and compared to him, other directors are just professional hackworkers earning a living.'

Again, this insistence on thinking of Kubrick in the present tense. On March 7, 1999, he died suddenly, much to everyone's surprise. Con Pederson says, 'I know he wasn't a young man anymore, but you got used to him being around. I guess we all thought he was immortal.'

**Grand hotel:**
*Kubrick lines up a shot of Dullea in the climactic bedroom scenes of the film.*

# further information:

**2001: A SPACE ODYSSEY**
**Arthur C. Clarke**
**based on the original screenplay by**
**Stanley Kubrick & Arthur C. Clarke (Hutchinson/Star, 1968)**
It always helps to read the novel, as much for the differences as for the similarities between book and film. Clarke's writing is often very poetic. Along with *Rendezvous with Rama,* this must by now have become one of the standard reference novels as far as space adventures within our own solar system are concerned.

**THE MAKING OF KUBRICK'S 2001**
**edited by Jerome Agel (New American Library, 1970)**
Paperback format, contains a ninety-page insert of small black-and-white stills from the movie, along with reprints of many reviews and articles. It's less about the 'making' of the movie, and rather more about critical reaction to it.

**THE LOST WORLDS OF 2001**
**Arthur C. Clarke (New American Library, 1972)**
Clarke's account of how the novel and script were written. Contains fascinating alternative chapters, plot developments and so forth. See also an essay contained in:

**REPORT ON PLANET THREE**
**Arthur C. Clarke (Victor Gollancz, 1973)**
*Son of Dr Strangelove*
Clarke recalls his first meeting with Kubrick and provides various anecdotes about his experiences on the film.

**ODYSSEY : The Authorized Biography of Arthur C. Clarke**
**Neil McAleer (Victor Gollancz, 1992)**
Accounts of Clarke's early life are sometimes surprising, often funny and touching. This is the story of a life well lived, even if it sometimes reads like a famous man's appointments diary rather than an analysis.

**AMERICAN CINEMATOGRAPHER**
**June 1968**
**Herb Lightman & Douglas Trumbull**
*Filming 2001: A Space Odyssey*
Definitive technical outline of special effects procedures aimed at professional film makers. Includes front projection, YCMs and mattes.

**AMERICAN CINEMATOGRAPHER**
**September 1968**
**Douglas Trumbull**
*The Slit-Scan Process*
A detailed guide to the slit-scan machine and its subsequent variations after *2001*, including a full description of the motors and controls.

**THE NEW YORKER**
**April 13, 1968**
**'The Current Cinema' (Penelope Gilliatt film review)**
*After Man*
Many thousands of reviews have been written on the theme of *2001*. This is by far the best (see pp: 64-65).

**STANLEY KUBRICK DIRECTS**
**Alexander Walker (Harcourt, 1972)**

*Recently revised and updated as:*

**STANLEY KUBRICK, DIRECTOR: A Visual Analysis**
**Alexander Walker (Weidenfeld & Nicholson, 1999)**
An eloquent and accessible guide to Kubrick's films. A valuable first primer under the helm of a well-respected British critic (with additional input from Sybil Taylor and Ulrich Ruchti).

**'IT'S ONLY A MOVIE, INGRID'**
**Alexander Walker (Headline Books, 1988)**
*Inexactly Expressed Sentiments...*
Fine examination of Kubrick as a human being. Walker isn't afraid to show his own awe and confusion, but works hard to demystify some of the more absurd legends that have sprung up about Kubrick.

**KUBRICK**
**Michel Ciment (English language version, William Collins, 1983)**
Despite occasional over-intellectualizing, French film academic Ciment has many very observant things to say about the themes running through Kubrick's work. Best of all, he interviews the director and some of his associates, Ken Adam and the late John Alcott among them.

**CINEFANTASTIQUE**
**June 1994**
**Dan Persons, Lowell Goldman, Steven Jongeward, Randall Larson**
*2001 Retrospective*
A wide-ranging 15-page celebration of the film, including interviews with Lockwood, Dullea, Trumbull and others; includes a feature on the late Alex North, composer of *2001*'s rejected orchestral score.

*The author also recommends a website containing a wide variety of materials, pictures, essays and links to other sites, compiled by Phil Vendy. "Underman's 2001" is at* **http://www.underview.com/2001.html**

# acknowledgements:

## the author would like to thank the following people for their very generous assistance:

Dr **ARTHUR C. CLARKE, O.B.E.** looked kindly on *Filming the Future* and agreed to contribute the foreword, as well as soliciting material from some of his friends and colleagues.

**FRED CLARKE** *(Arthur's brother in England)* supported *Filming the Future* in every way, and provided hundreds of documents and newspaper clippings. Thanks also to his charming wife **'BABS' CLARKE** who, together with Fred, made sure that Arthur heard the author's pleas for help. Personal assistant **CHRIS HOWSE** was constantly on hand, and knew where everything was.

**TONY FREWIN** *(at Mr Kubrick's office)* passed material and messages on my behalf to Kubrick during production of the first edition of this book, and has since provided valuable contacts for this new edition.

**HARRY LANGE** and **DAISY LANGE** spent many hours with the author talking about the film, and provided countless names and addresses. Harry described aspects of design in detail, and Daisy recounted many adventures during the making of *2001*.

**FRED ORDWAY** made documents and photos available from his archives and gave a detailed account of his work on the film.

**ROGER CARAS** provided invaluable information during long telephone conversations and in writing. Roger's *2001* deputy **IVOR POWELL** described daily life in Kubrick's production office.

**KEIR DULLEA** and **GARY LOCKWOOD** talked about their experiences on *2001*. **DOUGLAS TRUMBULL**, **CON PEDERSON**, **BRUCE LOGAN**, **BRYAN LOFTUS**, **BRIAN JOHNSON**, **ZORAN PERISIC** and **KEITH HAMSHERE** were tirelessly helpful, and all made archive documents and pictures available.

**ANDREW BIRKIN** told me about location stills photography for the *Dawn of Man* sequences, while **DAN RICHTER** and **KEITH DENNY** described what it was like to play apemen.

**HEATHER MASTERS** described her late husband Tony's work as Production Designer for *2001*. Thanks also to **GILES MASTERS**, Tony's son, for helping to locate other members of the *2001* Art Department.

**JOHN HOESLI** also told me about his and Masters' work on *2001*.

**ANNIE BOULAT** kindly supplied information about her late husband Pierre, who played a significant role in the *Dawn of Man* expedition.

**LAURIE BARR** *(contractor)* described the fabrication of various pieces of space hardware for *2001*.

**ARTHUR COLE** *(formerly of British Aerospace)* supplied technical items relating to Hawker Siddeley's work on the film.

**BOB CROWDEY** *(Technicolor, UK)* gave advice relating to his company's involvement in *2001*'s film processing.

**ALAN HERBERT** *(at the 3M Company, UK)* arranged sponsorship of exhibition expenses in relation to this book.

**JOHN JAY**, *2001*'s official publicity stills photographer, provided many wonderful pictures, and described working for Kubrick.

**MAT IRVINE** *(BBC Visual Effects)* for many useful items of material, and for putting me in touch with other effects experts.

**NEIL McALEER** *(Arthur Clarke's official biographer)* spoke about his work on the biography.

**DAVID HARDY** *(space artist)* provided many contacts.

**SIMON ATKINSON** *(artist and modelmaker)* recreated the main vehicles with great accuracy, after careful analysis of stills and photographs. His superb illustrations can be found within these pages.

**DENNIS GILLIAM** *(aerospace archivist)* deserves a special mention. He allowed unrestricted access to a wide selection of material from his collection, and flew to England from California to help out with the book. He also travelled widely in the USA to conduct research for the project.

Thanks also to: the **SPACE & ROCKET CENTER**, Huntsville, Alabama, the **NATIONAL MUSEUM OF SCIENCE & TECHNOLOGY**, London, the **BRITISH FILM INSTITUTE**, London, the **KOBAL COLLECTION**, London, the **RONALD GRANT ARCHIVE**, London, and the **SMITHSONIAN AIR & SPACE MUSEUM**, Washington, D.C.

*A Metro-Goldwyn-Mayer release*

# 2001: a space odyssey

produced and directed by
**STANLEY KUBRICK**

**Associate Producer**
VICTOR LYNDON

**Screenplay**
STANLEY KUBRICK & ARTHUR C. CLARKE

**Director of Photography**
GEOFFREY UNSWORTH

**Additional Photography**
JOHN ALCOTT

**Editor**
RAY LOVEJOY

**Camera Operator**
KELVIN PIKE

**Sound**
A.W. WATKINS

**Assistant Director**
DEREK CRACKNELL

**Production Design**
TONY MASTERS
HARRY LANGE
ERNIE ARCHER

**Scientific Adviser**
FREDERICK I. ORDWAY III

**Costumes**
HARDY AMIES

**Make-up**
STUART FREEBORN

**All Special Photographic Effects designed by**
STANLEY KUBRICK

Special Effects Supervisers
**WALLY VEEVERS    TOM HOWARD**
**DOUGLAS TRUMBULL    CON PEDERSON**
**COLIN CANTWELL    BRYAN LOFTUS**
**FREDERICK MARTIN    BRUCE LOGAN**
**JOHN JACK MALICK    DAVID OSBORNE**

cast
**KEIR DULLEA** *David Bowman*
**GARY LOCKWOOD** *Frank Poole*
**WILLIAM SYLVESTER** *Dr Heywood Floyd*
**DAN RICHTER** *Moonwatcher*
**DOUGLAS RAIN** *Voice of HAL 9000*
**LEONARD ROSSITER** *Dr Smyslov*
**MARGARET TYZACK** *Elena*
**ROBERT BEATTY** *Halvorsen*
**SEAN SULLIVAN** *Michaels*
**FRANK MILLER** *Mission Controller*
**PENNY BRAHMS** *Stewardess*
**VIVIAN KUBRICK** *Dr Floyd's daughter*

with
**ALAN GIFFORD, GLENN BECK, EDWINA CAROLL,**
**BILL WESTON, MIKE LOVELL, ANN GILLIS, ED BISHOP,**
**HEATHER DOWNHAM, JOHN ASHLEY, JIMMY BELL,**
**DAVID CHARKHAM, SIMON DAVIS, JONATHAN DAW,**
**PETER DELMAR, TERRY DUGGAN, DAVID FLEETWOOD,**
**DANNY GROVER, BRIAN HAWLEY, DAVID HINES,**
**TONY JACKSON, JOHN JORDAN, SCOTT MACKEE,**
**LAURENCE MARCHENT, DARRYL PAES, JOE REFALO,**
**ANDY WALLACE, BOB WILYMAN, RICHARD WOOD**

Music
*Gayaneh Ballet Suite* by Aram Katchaturian
*Atmospheres, Lux Aeterna, Requiem* by Gyorgy Ligeti
*The Blue Danube* by Johann Strauss
*Also Sprach Zarathustra* by Richard Strauss

filmed in 35mm & 70mm
**SUPER PANAVISION**

**TECHNICOLOR**
&
**METROCOLOR**

Distributed by
**METRO-GOLDWYN-MAYER**

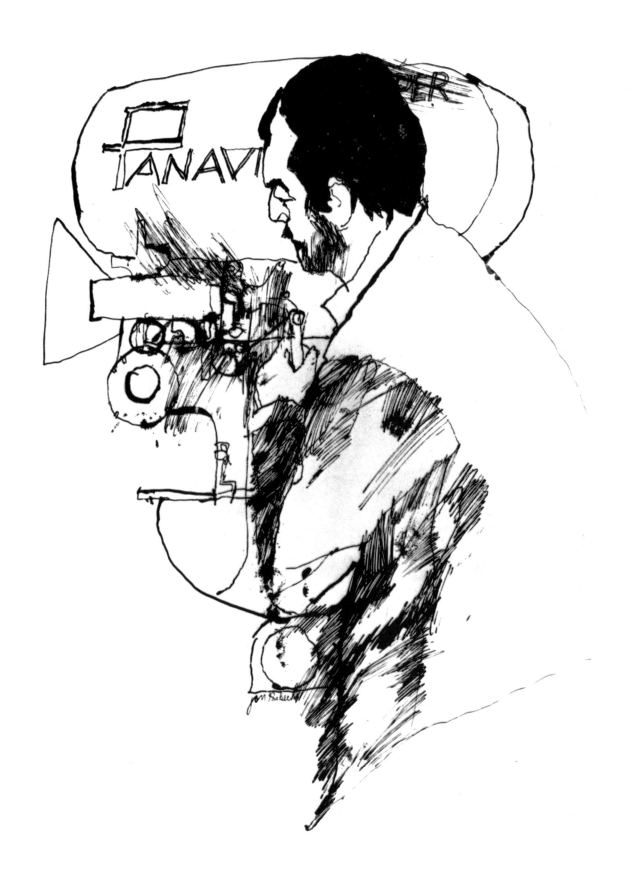